D0329632

BEST OF

Brussels, Bruges, Antwerp & Ghent

Terry Carter, Lara Dunston

How to use this book

Colour-Coding & Maps

Each chapter has a colour code along the banner at the top of the page which is also used for text and symbols on maps (eg all venues reviewed in the Highlights chapter are orange on the maps). The fold-out maps inside the front and back covers are numbered from 1 to 8. Most sights and venues in the text have map references; eg, (3, B2) means Map 3, grid reference B2. See p128 for map symbols.

Prices

Multiple prices listed with reviews (eg €10/5) usually indicate adult/concession admission to a venue, and €10/3/5 adult/child/concession. Concession prices can include senior, student, member or coupon discounts. Meal cost and room rate categories are listed in the Directory chapter (p113).

Text Symbols

- ☎ telephone
- ✉ address
- 🖳 email/website address
- € admission
- ☺ opening hours
- ⓘ information
- Ⓜ metro
- 🚌 bus
- 🚃 premetro, tram
- ♿ wheelchair access
- 🍴 on site/nearby eatery
- 👶 child-friendly venue
- Ⓥ good vegetarian selection

Best of Brussels, Bruges, Antwerp & Ghent
1st edition – September 2006

Published by Lonely Planet Publications Pty Ltd
ABN 36 005 607 983

Australia Head Office, Locked Bag 1, Footscray, Vic 3011
☎ 03 8379 8000, fax 03 8379 8111
🖳 talk2us@lonelyplanet.com.au

USA 150 Linden St, Oakland, CA 94607
☎ 510 893 8555, toll free 800 275 8555
fax 510 893 8572
🖳 info@lonelyplanet.com

UK 72–82 Rosebery Ave, Clerkenwell, London EC1R 4RW
☎ 020 7841 9000, fax 020 7841 9001
🖳 go@lonelyplanet.co.uk

This title was commissioned in Lonely Planet's London office and produced by: **Commissioning Editors** Meg Worby & Tashi Wheeler **Coordinating Editor** Barbara Delissen **Coordinating Cartographer** Matthew Kelly **Layout Designer** Jacqueline McLeod **Editor** Margedd Heliosz **Cartographer** Malisa Plesa **Managing Cartographer** Mark Griffiths **Cover Designer** Jim Hsu **Project Manager** Eoin Dunlevy **Mapping Development** Paul Piaia **Desktop Publishing Support** Mark Germanchis **Thanks to** Imogen Bannister, Adrienne Costanzo, Sally Darmody, Kate McDonald, Glenn van der Knijff, Wibowo Rusli, Celia Wood

Photographs by Lonely Planet Images Jean-Bernard Carillet & Terry Carter, except for the following: p5, 61 Juliet Coombe; p8, p55 John Elk III; p34, p68 Rick Gerharter; p8, p10, p24, p50, p50, p67, p80 Leanne Logan; p67 Diana Mayfield; p33, p48, p75, p78 Doug McKinlay; p19, p21, p24, p57, p56, p59, p59, p66, p81 Martin Moos; p13, p38, p65 Wayne Walton. **Cover photograph** Guildhouse on Grand Place, Brussels, Pat Behnke/Photolibrary. All images are copyright of the photographers unless otherwise indicated. Many of the images in this guide are available for licensing from Lonely Planet Images: www.lonelyplanetimages.com.

ISBN 1 74059 739 7

Printed through The Bookmaker International Ltd.
Printed in China

Acknowledgements Brussels Transit Map © STIB/MIVB 2006

Contents

From the Publisher

AUTHORS
Terry Carter

A musician as much as a writer-photographer, it was the gypsy jazz chords of Django Reinhardt that initially drew Terry's attention to Belgium. A fanatical cook, *moules et frites* were the first words out of his mouth when arriving in Brussels and he's been hooked since. After more than a decade working in Sydney's publishing industry designing books and websites, Terry moved to the United Arab Emirates in 1998 with partner Lara and has since travelled extensively throughout the Middle East and Europe. Terry has a Master's degree in media studies and divides his time between freelance travel writing, photography and web design.

Lara Dunston

Lara's love for Belgian cinema (Chantal Ackerman, Dardenne brothers) began before she realised they were Belgian! Two decades later, she appreciates these adventurous talents couldn't be anything but Flemish and has added Antwerp fashion and anything Art Nouveau to her list of Belgian passions. With degrees in film, international studies and screenwriting, since the late '80s Lara's had careers in filmmaking, politics, writing and media education, and has travelled to over 50 countries, living away from her native Australia for nine years in South America and the Middle East, including time in Brussels.

LONELY PLANET AUTHORS
Why is our travel information the best in the world? It's simple: our authors are independent, dedicated travellers. They don't research using just the Internet or phone, and they don't take freebies in exchange for positive coverage. They travel widely, to all the popular spots and off the beaten track. They personally visit thousands of hotels, restaurants, cafés, bars, galleries, palaces, museums and more – and they take pride in getting all the details right, and telling it how it is. For more, see the authors section on **www.lonelyplanet.com**.

PHOTOGRAPHERS
Jean-Bernard Carillet

A Paris-based author and photographer, Jean-Bernard has contributed to numerous LP guides. When not shooting crystal-clear lagoons in the tropics or markets in Africa, he goes regularly to eastern France, southern Belgium and the Ruhr in Germany to work on a darker subject – the remaining industrial wasteland.

Terry Carter

Terry Carter studied reportage photography at university while doing a communications degree. While still loving the look, he doesn't miss the chemical smells and isolation of the darkroom and now edits his photos on planes, trains and ships while travelling. His photography has featured in several travel magazines.

SEND US YOUR FEEDBACK
We love to hear from travellers – your comments keep us on our toes and help make our books better. Our well-travelled team reads every word on what you loved or loathed about this book. Although we cannot reply individually to postal submissions, we always guarantee that your feedback goes straight to the appropriate authors, in time for the next edition – and the most useful submissions are rewarded with a free book. To send us your updates – and find out about Lonely Planet events, newsletters and travel news – visit our award-winning website: **www.lonelyplanet.com/feedback**.

Note: We may edit, reproduce and incorporate your comments in Lonely Planet products such as guidebooks, websites and digital products, so let us know if you don't want your comments reproduced or your name acknowledged. For a copy of our privacy policy visit **www.lonelyplanet.com/privacy**.

Boring. Bureaucratic. Bland. To many, this is how Brussels (Bruxelles in French, Brussel in Flemish) is perceived. The reality is Brussels is far more interesting than a Eurocrat's press conference. This capital of Europe is not just an empty figurehead, Brussels is a lively, down-to-earth European capital, with transcendent Art Nouveau buildings, fashion houses working out of petite shopfronts and sidewalk cafés where a reluctant sun is savoured along with the world's best beers.

It's not until you've wandered around this eminently walkable city, however, that you build a picture of its true nature. Once you've done the Grand Place and its beautiful old guildhouses, head further afield along the cobbled streets. Turning nearly every corner reveals a cartoon-themed mural, often amusingly tailored to its surroundings. Local bars lure you in with the promise of a new brew to sample. Waiters balancing potfuls of steaming mussels skilfully weave past you on their way to a table full of locals having a long working lunch.

Truth is, Brussels is a far more relaxed place than its political status would indicate – and a lot less strait-laced. What city could elevate Manneken Pis – the statue of a little boy peeing – to iconic status? Who else would name a beer 'Mort Subite' (sudden death)? And where else would the whimsical journeys of reporter Tintin have been able to blossom into one of the most loved comic characters in the world? While it's all business and bureaucrats on the surface, there's far more to Brussels than meets the eye.

Smile for the camera: a Frank Pé mural on Rue Plattesteen

Brussels' old centre is divided into two main areas, the Lower Town and the Upper Town, surrounded by a series of connecting boulevards referred to as the *petit* (small) ring, while the city itself is surrounded by a larger ring road.

The **Lower Town** is Brussels' compact medieval core with the magnificent Grand Place as its ancient centrepiece. Northwest of Grand Place is **Ilôt Sacré**, with cobblestone streets lined with tourist restaurants and old pubs hidden down narrow alleyways, while to the west, beyond the elegant Bourse (stock exchange), is the stylish area of **St-Géry**, full of designer boutiques and atmospheric bars, and charming **Ste-Catherine**, with its seafood market and wonderful restaurants. In the surrounding streets towards the canal is a colourful Moroccan neighbourhood and an arty, alternative feel to some streets. A small area centred on Rue du Marché au Charbon is home to the city's gay community, with lively bars and cabarets. In the Lower Town's southwest is working-class **Marolles**, with rowdy local pubs, cluttered bric-a-brac shops, and a daily flea market.

The aristocratic **Upper Town** weighs heavy with grand palaces, elegant mansions and wide boulevards. The city's finest museums, a tranquil park and embassies are here. To the southwest is the **Sablon**, with antique shops and outdoor cafés, and Ave Louise with its exclusive stores.

East of the centre, off Ave Louise, is the affluent area of **Ixelles** and neighbouring **St-Gilles** whose streets are home to Art Nouveau architecture and superb restaurants. North of Ixelles, around Porte de Namur, is the vibrant **Matongé** district, home to Brussels' African community and cheap atmospheric eateries. Heading north is the dull **EU area**, dominated by the ugly European Parliament and administrative buildings, with little to interest visitors. North of this are ethnic **St-Josse** and **Schaerbeek**, with a lively Turkish neighbourhood centred around Chaussée de Haecht. Beyond this is leafy **Laeken** and the Belgian royal estate. West and southwest are the peaceful suburbs of **Molenbeek-St-Jean** and **Anderlecht**.

OFF THE BEATEN TRACK

To escape the crowds, slip away to:
- the welcome foliage of Forêt de Soignes (p23)
- the Art Nouveau backstreets of St-Gilles and Ixelles (p37)
- the duck pond on Square Marie-Louise (p23)

A skatepark in Marolles

TERRY CARTER

Itineraries Brussels

One Day

Hit some vibrant cultural spaces and museums such as **BOZAR** (p18), **Musées Royaux des Beaux-Arts de Belgique** (p15) and the **Musée des Instruments de Musique** (p16), then do our Atmospheric Amble (p102), a café-bar hop that takes in the splendid **Grand Place** (p8), elegant **Galeries Royales** (p28), flamboyant cafés, characterful bars, and traditional restaurants.

Two Days

Browse **Marolles flea market** (3, C6), listen to gypsy jazz at **La Brocante** (p44) and have a traditional meal at **Brasserie Ploegmans** (p39) or explore the Rue Antoine Dansaert fashion area and have modern tapas at **Le Fourneau** (p40) or seafood at **Ste-Catherine** (p40). In the afternoon have a giggle at the **Centre Belge de la Bande Dessinée** (p14), then check out Brussels' murals with our Mural Mosey walk (p103). Dine at one of the many bistros in lively **Matongé** or **Ixelles** (p37), catch jazz at **Sounds** (p47), a live concert at **Ancienne Belgique** (p47), or save yourself for after-midnight clubbing at **Dirty Dancing** (p46).

WORST OF BRUSSELS
- Risking your life each time you cross the road.
- Dog droppings – giving Paris a run for its poop.
- Open men's urinals – we're not sure if it's the sight, sound or smell that's worse!
- The predictably unpredictable weather.

One Week

With a week, visit hip **Antwerp** (p75) for a couple of days, laid-back **Ghent** (p94) for a day, and leave two days for pretty **Bruges** (p61). In each city, do our walks first, then spend some time experiencing the wonderful sights, culinary delights, atmospheric cafés, convivial bars and funky clubs we've chosen in each place.

Grand guildhouses on the Grand Place

TERRY CARTER

GRAND PLACE (4, D5)

A truly magnificent sight, Grand Place's astounding baroque and Gothic shapes are etched into every visitor's memory (and their memory cards) on first visit. Once the economic and political heart of Brussels, today the square echoes to the footsteps of teeming masses of tourists, but the façades of the guildhalls still transcend.

INFORMATION

- ✉ Grand Place, Lower Town
- Ⓜ De Brouckère
- 🚇 Bourse
- ♿ fair
- 🍴 't Kelderke (p36)

JOHN ELK III

Once marshland, cobblestones were first laid in the 12th century and the square used as a Grote Markt (marketplace) – hence the surrounding streets' names, such as Rue des Bouchers (Butchers Street). The square's position as the city's focal point was emphasised by the building of the Gothic **Hôtel de Ville** (town hall, built 1401–59), with its beautifully detailed façade.

The majority of the guildhalls in the square date from the end of the 17th century (below). The **Maison des Boulangers** (meaning 'Bakers' House'; No 1) was once the bakers' guild, but today is home to bar Le Roy d'Espagne (p45). **Le Cornet** (The Horn; No 6) is easily identifiable as the home of the boatmen's guild by its stern-shaped top floor, while next door, **Le Renard** (The Fox) housed the haberdashers' guild. **Le Cygne** (The Swan; No 9) hosted the butchers' guild and later a workers' café frequented by Karl Marx.

The bust-lined building at the square's southeastern end is **La Maison des Ducs de Brabant** (The House of the Dukes of Brabant) and comprises half a dozen neoclassical guildhalls. Another prominent building is the **Maison du Roi** (King's House), now home to the Musée de la Ville de Bruxelles (p20).

LEANNE LOGAN

QUICK-FIRE RENOVATIONS

The guildhouses on the Grand Place are not the originals. On 13 August 1695, France's Louis XIV began a 36-hour cannonball bombardment of Grand Place from beyond the city walls, with only the Hôtel de Ville and two guildhalls surviving the assault. The indefatigable Bruxellois rebuilt the square in fantastic Flemish Renaissance style within five years.

BEER

Beer (*bière* in French, *bier* in Flemish) in Belgium is a seriously fun business. While it's treated as earnestly as wine in France, it's a far more egalitarian pursuit here, although with around 600 brews on offer, Belgian beer can seem as intimidating as a French wine list. Start your beer quest by sipping the 'Trappist' beers, the holy grail of Belgian beers. Several Trappist monasteries have close associations with their yeasty products – Chimay, Orval, Rochefort, Westmalle and Westvleteren beers for example – and all are characterised by a gold or dark colour, a strong, smooth taste, and an alcohol content upwards of 6%. Abbey beers (made under license) are not the same as Trappist, but try a Leffe just the same.

TERRY CARTER

DON'T MISS
- Drinking in a classic café such as À la Mort Subite (p43) or Art Nouveau wonder Falstaff (p44)
- Tasting a Westmalle Tripel, Orval, Duvel and Cantillon Gueuze
- Taking home a set of Trappist beers (and matching glasses) from De Biertempel (p33)
- Checking out the **Belgian Brewers Museum** (4, D6; ☎ 02 511 49 87; Grand Place 10; admission €4; ⏰ 10am-5pm daily Apr-Nov, from noon Sat & Sun Dec-Mar)

TERRY CARTER

White beers (*bière blanche* in French or *witbier* in Flemish) are pale and cloudy wheat or barley beers with a relatively low alcohol content (4% to 5.5%) and are refreshing during summer – try a Hoegaarden. Belgium's lager-style brews such as the ubiquitous Stella Artois are good summer tipples as well. Stronger ales, such as delicious Duvel (Devil – 8.5%) make great winter beers, as does Bush beer, which – at just under 12% – will ensure plenty of Christmas spirit!

The most interesting beers produced, however, are the unique lambics (or *lambiek* in Flemish), which are barrel fermented for up to four years. There are different types, including fruit versions such as *kriek* (made with cherries) and *framboise* (made with raspberries), but the best brew is the dry, slightly bitter *gueuze* – try Cantillon. These fizzy brews actually come with a cork – just like champagne.

CHOCOLATE

Chocolates are as synonymous with Belgium as beer is – Belgians are master-craftsmen and connoisseurs of both, and most travellers leave Brussels airport laden with Westmalles and Wittamers, Leffes and Leonidas. All Belgian chocolate is fine and Belgians would take to the streets to protest anything less.

Belgian chocolate houses have passed their recipes down through several generations and keep them closely guarded secrets. Belgians gave us the praline. Developed by the Neuhaus family in Brussels in 1912, it was the first filled chocolate. Containing the smoothest textures of nuts, nougat, honeycomb etc, it's covered with high-quality dark, milk or white chocolate.

Unfortunately, while Belgian chocolate is a taste sensation, its history leaves a bitter taste in your mouth, tied as it is to Belgium's acquisition of the Congo, which facilitates easy access to Africa's cocoa fields and lead to spectacular growth of the chocolate manufacturing industry. Like many Belgian chocolates, the Cote d'Or was first made in 1885 when elephants transported cocoa beans through the tropical jungle, hence the elephant on the packaging. When King Léopold II colonised the Congo, as well as taking advantage of their cocoa beans, he committed the first genocide of the twentieth century – around ten million were killed under Léopold's orders. Arguably the best cocoa beans in the world grow in the Congo, but while the area is now war-ravaged, Belgium maintains its cocoa importing links.

DON'T MISS
- Visiting the **Musée du Cacao et du Chocolat** (4, D6; ☎ 02 514 20 48; Grand Place 13 ▢ www.mucc.be; €5/free/4; ☹ 10am-5pm Tue-Sun) to learn how chocolate travelled to Europe, checking out the wonderful old chocolate boxes and salivating chocolate-making demonstrations
- Buying Belgian chocolates – try Godiva, Wittamer, Neuhaus – they're all divine, and cheaper than they are back home
- Trying a warm chocolate-coated waffle…yum

Hard to resist

STE-CATHERINE & ST-GÉRY (4, B2 & B3)

The charming laid-back neighbourhoods of Ste-Catherine and St-Géry may comprise Brussels' oldest quarters, yet today they are the most contemporary and cutting-edge areas.

Brussels was founded on the site of Place St-Géry. In 977 the area was part of the duchy of Lower Lotharingia, given by emperor Otto II to Charles, the banished son of King Louis IV of France. However, it wasn't until 979 – when Charles built a small castle on St-Géry island, at the time surrounded by the Senne river – that Brussels was born.

While the Senne river was long ago covered or filled to prevent disease spreading, St-Géry and Ste-Catherine have remained islands in many ways, the centres of cutting-edge fashion and design, quality cuisine, contemporary culture and hip nightlife. They are surrounded by more conservative neighbourhoods, both traditional Bruxellois and immigrant families from the Middle East, Africa, Latin America and East Asia.

Here you'll discover adventurous performing arts theatres, bookshops specialising in poetry, design and art, young fashion graduates cutting their own patterns in the backroom ateliers of their chic boutiques, and inspiring chefs serving cuisine that experiments with traditional recipes. But you'll also find specialist seafood merchants and mushroom vendors (trading the fresh produce in the way their ancestors did), old men playing chess in the local pub, Muslim mothers walking their children home from school and Indian immigrants borrowing Bollywood tapes from a local video store. It's this close juxtaposition of Belgian and 'other', traditional and modern, that makes it so exciting.

INFORMATION

- ✉ Lower Town
- Ⓜ Ste Catherine
- 🚊 Bourse
- ♿ good
- 🍴 Le Fourneau (p40)

JEAN-BERNARD CARILLET

DON'T MISS

- Marvelling at the Maison de la Bellone (p21)
- Visiting designer ateliers – you could be buying from 'the next big thing'
- Snapping a pic of the canine version of Manneken Pis: 'Zinneke Pis' (p25)

MUSÉE ROYAL DE L'AFRIQUE CENTRALE (2, D2)

Once controversial due to its inception, following the World Fair in 1897, as the Musée du Congo, a colonial showpiece that promoted the allegedly idealistic nature of the Congo 'Free' State founded by Léopold II in 1885, the museum is currently renovating and refocusing its exhibitions to acknowledge its colonial history.

INFORMATION

☎ 02 769 52 11

🖥 www.africamuseum.be

✉ Leuvensesteenweg 13, Tervuren

€ €4/free/1.50/3

🕑 10am-5pm Tue-Fri, 10am-6pm Sat & Sun

ⓘ most labelling in French and Flemish, but increasingly English is being added

Ⓜ Montgomery, then tram 44 to Tervuren terminus, then a 300m walk

♿ excellent

JEAN-BERNARD CARILLET

The tyrannical Léopold II colonized the Congo in 1885, a territory 86 times bigger than Belgium. He spent two decades plundering ivory, rubber and cocoa beans, generating immense wealth through slavery, and using the riches to fund building projects in Brussels – such as that of the museum.

The museum's unique collections allow an extraordinary insight into central African societies and natural environments, through its (often kitsch) dioramas and displays of artefacts. There are exhibitions on prehistory, zoology (including an enormous stuffed elephant), agriculture and forestry, geology and mineralogy. Highlights include the fascinating ethnographic section with its mind-boggling collection of masks, musical instruments, jewellery, decorative arts, a huge dugout canoe (pirogue) and myriad artefacts impossible to see elsewhere outside Africa. There's room for improvement in the history displays that document Belgian 'exploration', colonisation and Christianisation, although there are wonderful artefacts, such as Henry Morton Stanley's travelling trunk and vibrant African art.

AN INFORMED VIEW

King Leopold's Ghost (Adam Hochschild) examines Léopold II's disturbing Central African land-grab and how he sold the idea to the world, without revealing his true intentions, with help from luminaries such as explorer Henry Morton Stanley.

Already a respected international research institute, the museum aims to become a meeting place and centre for intercultural dialogue and exchange. Through photographs, films and documents, the 'historical walk' helps visitors understand the collection from a historical perspective. There is a good café serving African dishes, and the museum shop has some fabulous jewellery, textiles and art.

CATHÉDRALE DES STS MICHEL & GUDULE (3, E3)

This imposing, solemn twin-towered church, constructed over three centuries from 1226 is a splendid sight, especially with its atmospheric lighting at night. Originally a chapel dedicated to St-Michel, as early as the 9th century, it was replaced by a Romanesque church in the 11th century. The relics of St-Gudule were transferred there and the church was dedicated to Brussels' male and female patron saints, Michel and Gudule, respectively.

The church that we see today is a classic of Brabant Gothic architecture, built with the orders of Henry I, Duke of Brabant. Inside the cathedral, perhaps the most obvious sign the church has undergone the odd renovation over the years is the great organ of the cathedral taking up a rather conspicuous position on the left. While the instrument, installed in 2000, has impressive specifications (a total of 4300 pipes, 63 stops, four keyboards and a pedal board), it sits rather oddly opposite the beautiful baroque pulpit, carved by Henri-François Verbruggen in 1699 in Antwerp, and depicting Adam and Eve's hurried exit from Eden.

Light streams into the voluminous church through some very impressive stained-glass windows, several made by Jean Haeck, a master glass worker from Antwerp, in 1537. After the last renovation between 1983 and 1999, a new high altar was commissioned and placed at the crossing of the transept. This intriguing granite sculpture adds yet another layer of complexity to this unique church.

INFORMATION

☎ 02 217 83 45
🖳 www.cathedralestmichel.be
✉ Parvis Ste Gudule, Upper Town
€ treasury €1; Romanesque ruins donation €1
🕐 treasury 10am-12.30pm & 2-5pm
ℹ organ concerts usually held 8pm Tue
Ⓜ Gare Centrale
♿ fair
🍴 Aux Armes de Bruxelles (p35)

WAYNE WALTON

DON'T MISS

- The beautifully elaborate oak confessionals
- The close-up details of the baroque pulpit
- The gargoyles that decorate the exterior
- The ruins of the early church (downstairs to the left after you enter the cathedral)

JEAN-BERNARD CARILLET

CENTRE BELGE DE LA BANDE DESSINÉE (3, E3)

Illustrated stories have been inspiring, humouring, and capturing the imaginations of Belgian and foreign comic enthusiasts for nearly a century, and the Belgian Centre for Comic Strip Art, or Comic Strip Museum, is a wonderful showcase for Belgium's favourite art. Occupying the splendid Grand Magasin Waucquez, a 1906 Art Nouveau department store created by Victor Horta and painstakingly restored, this extensive collection displays work by some of Belgium's best-loved comic artists.

The upstairs galleries trace the origins of Belgian comic-strip art, from the first Tintin publication (*Tintin au Pays des Soviets;* Tintin in the Land of the Soviets) by Hergé in 1929, to the post-WWII creation of *Suske en Wiske* (Bob and Bobette) by Willy Vandersteen, Morris' Wild West cowboy parody *Lucky Luke* and the loveable little blue and white creatures that creator Peyo (aka Pierre Culliford) called Le Schtroumpf, but became known as the Smurfs in English.

The top level is devoted to comic strips from the 1960s onwards and contains works of social satire and thrilling science fiction and fantasy stories. While part of the exhibition illustrates how comic strips are assembled, die-hard fans and aspiring comic book artists will crave more preliminary sketches and original artwork. The avant-garde and edgier comics are also ignored in favour the more mainstream strips. On the other hand, those new to the art may find the exhibition overwhelming – having few labels in English doesn't help either, although there's an English-language booklet you can borrow from the ticket counter on the way in. The gift shop is excellent.

INFORMATION

- ☎ 02 219 19 80
- 🖳 www.stripmuseum.be
- ✉ Rue des Sables 20, Lower Town
- € €7.5/3/6
- 🕒 10am-6pm Tue-Sun
- ⓘ free English-language folder available at reception
- Ⓜ Gare Centrale
- ♿ fair
- ✕ Horta Brasserie Restaurant (p35)

TERRY CARTER

LES CITÉS OBSCURES

Les Cités Obscures (www.urbicande.be) by artist François Schuiten and author Benoît Peeters is a fantastic epic of strange parallel-universe cities, that includes the story Brüsel, whose reality-based overriding theme is the EU's domination of Brussels.

MUSÉES ROYAUX DES BEAUX-ARTS DE BELGIQUE (3, D5)

Enjoying the exceptional collections of artworks of the Royal Museums of Fine Arts of Belgium – stretched across several museums – is high on many visitors' list of things to do in Brussels. It's comprised of four separate museums: the Museum of Ancient Art, established in 1801, with paintings and sculptures dating up to the 19th century; the Museum of Modern Art, which started in 1984 and spans the 20th century; the Wiertz Museum (p19), displaying the work of the Belgian romantic painter, which became part of the Royal Museums in 1868; and the Meunier Museum (p20), the home-studio of Constantin Meunier, acquired in 1939.

INFORMATION
- ☎ 02 508 32 11
- 🖳 www.fine-arts-museum.be
- ✉ Rue de la Régence 3 (Ancient) & Place Royale 102 (Modern)
- € €5/2/3.50; audio guides €2.50
- ⏲ 10am-5pm Tue-Sun
- ⓘ certain sections close daily between 12-1pm and 1-2pm
- Ⓜ Parc
- ♿ excellent
- 🍽 on-site café

Highlights of the Museum of Ancient Art are paintings from the 15th and 16th centuries, including Flemish primitives, Hans Memling, Rogier Van der Weyden, Dirk Bouts and a whole room dedicated to Hieronymus Bosch (but unfortunately Bosch' *Triptyque de la Tentation de Saint Antoine* is a copy).

Rubens dominates the 17th- and 18th-century collection, including the magnificent *Adoration of the Magi*, although you'll also get to appreciate fantastic pieces by Bruegel the Elder and Antoon Van Dyck.

The rich 19th-century exhibition covers Romanticism, Orientalism, Impressionism, Post-Impressionism, and includes wonderful work by Paul Gauguin, Pierre Bonnard and James Ensor. The highlight for many, however, is the 20th century with its spectacular collection of Surrealism, and work by Paul Delvaux, Giorgio de Chirico, and the largest collection of Magrittes in one place anywhere.

There's also a lovely sculpture garden, a decent café and an excellent bookshop.

Enjoy the heights of Belgian art

MUSÉE DES INSTRUMENTS DE MUSIQUE (4, E4)

This magical musical instrument museum, also known as MIM, has a brilliant collection of over 1500 instruments housed in a classic Art Nouveau building. The exhibition spans several floors and several centuries and music lovers will need at least three hours to do the museum justice. Even if you're not a music-lover, the building, designed by Paul Saintenoy and dating from 1898–99, is worth a visit alone. A former department store named 'Old England', it has been beautifully restored – if you see photos of the building from the 1980s you'll note the turret on the corner of the building was missing.

INFORMATION

☎ 02 545 01 30

▢ www.mim.fgov.be

✉ Rue Montagne de la Cour 2, Upper Town

€ €5/free/3.50

🕙 9.30am-5pm Tue, Wed & Fri, 9.30am-8pm Thu, 10am-5pm Sat & Sun

ⓘ there is a great bookshop on the ground floor

Ⓜ Gare Centrale

♿ excellent

🍴 6th-floor café

JEAN-BERNARD CARILLET

Four storeys of the building are dedicated to the museum. On the ground floor there are displays of folk instruments from Belgium, Europe and beyond. Downstairs on level -1 there are displays of 20th-century and mechanical instruments, including the ondes Martenot which was invented in 1928 and recently used extensively by Radiohead's resident genius Jonny Greenwood. The first floor starts a fascinating progression of Western instruments through the ages, and the second floor concentrates on keyboards and stringed instruments, with some very beautiful harps on display.

While there are plenty of instruments in glass cases, the headphones provided automatically trigger sound samples of many of the instruments and this works especially well on the first floor where the audible progression of instruments adds greatly to the experience. When you're done, head up to the 6th-floor café, even if you're not hungry – the views are sublime.

DON'T MISS

- Checking out the inventions of Adolphe Sax
- Admiring the detail of the gorgeous 16th-century harpsichords
- Seeing if there's a performance on (5th floor) while you're in Brussels
- Taking in the iron and glass beauty of the building's exterior from across the road

JEAN-BERNARD CARILLET

MUSÉE HORTA (6, A2)

Situated in St-Gilles, considered along with Ixelles to be the cradle of Belgian Art Nouveau, the Horta Museum is a wonderful showcase for the graceful and supple style of Brussels' architectural pioneer, Victor Horta.

Aimed at breaking away from styles of the past to create a style that better reflected the society at the time, Art Nouveau was adopted by more progressive architects with aspirations to embellish the built environment, particularly workers' homes, for aesthetic and moral reasons. Victor Horta's aims were also philanthropic, and in addition to his designs for middle class mansions, he created kindergartens, hospitals and a railway station.

Hôtel Tassel, Horta's first creation, was revealed in 1893 and was followed by such Art Nouveau masterpieces as the Hôtel Solvay, the Maison du Peuple (the former headquarters of the Socialist Party that was sadly torn down in 1965) and the Grand Magasin Waucquez

INFORMATION
- ☎ 02 543 04 90
- 🖥 www.hortamuseum.be
- ✉ Rue Américaine 25, St-Gilles
- € €7.50/2.50/3.50
- 🕑 2-5.30pm Tue-Sun
- ℹ guidebook and guided tours
- 🚋 Horta; 91 or 92 from Place Louise
- ✕ Le Fils de Jules or Quincaillerie (p37)

(now the Centre Belge de la Bande Dessinée; p14). Horta built himself a home and studio between 1898 and 1901, on Rue Américaine, where he would live and work for 20 years, and which is now this stunning museum, one of Brussels' most popular.

DON'T MISS
- The detail on the exterior balconies
- Intricately patterned wallpapers
- The cupboard urinal in the 1st-floor bedroom!

Victor Horta's splendid style and attention to detail can be seen all over the building, from the fabulous furniture and spectacular stained-glass skylights to the beautiful banisters, doorknobs and light fittings. Horta's diary detailing his intricate planning and execution, step-by-step, offers a fascinating account and insight for aspiring architects and builders.

Horta's Art Nouveau museum in all its glory

JEAN-BERNARD CARILLET

MUSEUMS & GALLERIES

Autoworld

This museum in Parc du Cinquantenaire is strictly one for car buffs. It consists of three private collections: one of motor vehicles, one of two-wheelers and a collection of coaches and carriages. There's also a section dedicated to auto design over the last 100 years or so, often featuring recent concept cars.

☎ 02 736 41 65 ⌨ www .autoworld.be ✉ Parc du Cinquantenaire 11, EU Area € €6/3/4.70 ⏲ 10am-6pm Tue-Sun Apr-Sep, 10am-5pm Tue-Sun Oct-Mar Ⓜ Mérode ♿ fair

Ye olde cars at Autoworld

JEAN-BERNARD CARILLET

BELvue Museum (3, E4)

Occupying a former late 18th-century luxury hotel and royal residence, this compelling Museum on Belgian History uses fascinating photos, films, historical documents and objects from everyday life to engage visitors with key historical periods, from the popular uprising of 1830 to the two world wars. Don't miss the archaeological ruins of the 11th-century Coudenberg Palace, the ancient palace of Charles V.

☎ 02 545 08 00 ⌨ www .belvue.be ✉ Place des

Palais 7, Upper Town € BELvue €3/free/2; Coudenberg €4/free/3; BELvue & Coudenberg €5/free/4 ⏲ 10am-6pm Tue-Sun Jun-Sep, 10am-5pm Tue-Sun Oct-May Ⓜ Parc ♿ fair

BOZAR (3, E4)

This vibrant arts and cultural space, also known as the Palais des Beaux Arts, is a magnanimous host to myriad performing arts events, exciting exhibitions on art, photography, decorative arts and design.

☎ 02 507 82 00 ⌨ www .bozar.be ✉ Rue Ravenstein 23 € varies depending on exhibition/event ⏲ 10am-6pm Tue-Sun Apr-Sep, 10am-5pm Tue-Sun Oct-Mar,

to 9pm Thu year-round Ⓜ Parc ♿ fair

Bruxella 1238 (4, C4)

Municipal workers accidentally discovered these underground remains of a 13th-century Franciscan convent beneath the Bourse in 1988. Check out the ruins through glass in front of Le Cirio, or head downstairs for a closer look.

☎ 02 279 43 50 ✉ Rue de la Bourse, Lower Town € €3 ⏲ 11.15am & 3pm 1st Wed of month Ⓜ De Brouckère Ⓑ Bourse

Cinquantenaire Museum

An incredible 350,000 artefacts from all continents, spanning antiquity, national archaeology, non-European civilizations and European arts and crafts make up the permanent collection at the majestic Royal Museum of Art and History. We love the fine jewellery and cult of the dead funerary gifts from the Merovingian civilisation.

☎ 02 741 72 11 ⌨ www .mrah.be ✉ Parc du

STREET TALK

You'll notice on street signs that Brussels has some peculiarly long street names, along the lines of 'Petite Rue de la Violette Korte Violetstraat'. This is because each sign includes both the French and Dutch names, with the French name coming first. Also note that the French *rue* (street) comes at the start of a name, while the Dutch *straat* is at the end.

Cinquantenaire 10, EU Area € permanent collection €4/1.50/3, Horta-Lambeaux Pavilion €2 ⏱ 9.30am-5pm Tue-Fri, 10am-5pm Sat & Sun Ⓜ Mérode ♿ good

Fondation Jacques Brel
(3, D4)
Initially rejected by the Belgians, Brussels-born Jacques Brel shone in Paris – his moving lyrics about the working-class helped make him one of Europe's most successful singer-songwriters. Set up by his daughter, this interactive museum screens his extraordinary final concert and various other films and sells his recordings.
☎ 02 511 10 20 ✉ Place de la Vieille Halle aux Blés, Lower Town € €5/free/3.50 ⏱ 11am-5pm Tue-Sat Ⓜ De Brouckère 🚋 Bourse

Maison d'Erasme
While Dutch humanist scholar Erasmus (1466?–1536) only lived here for five months in 1521, this lovely gabled house-museum with splendid portraits by Flemish primitives, 16th-century editions of his books, a cast of his skull and a tranquil sculpture garden, is a good excuse to get out of the centre. It can be visited with a combined ticket for nearby **Musée du Béguinage** (Rue du Chapelain 8, Anderlecht).
☎ 02 521 13 83 ✉ Rue du Chapitre 31, Anderlecht € €1.25 incl admission to Musée du Béguinage ⏱ 10am-5pm Tue-Sun Ⓜ St-Guidon

Musée Antoine Wiertz
Antoine-Joseph Wiertz' former studio is home to the

Erasmus himself

19th-century painter, sculptor and writer's dramatic and often monumental canvases, such as *The Greeks and the Trojans Claiming the Body of Patrocles*.
☎ 02 648 17 18 ✉ Rue Vautier 62, EU Area € free

SAVING ON SIGHTS
The Brussels Card (€30) is excellent value, giving free admission for 72 hours to 25 participating museums (including almost all the ones we've covered here), free rides on public transport, 25% discounts in other tourist attractions, shops, restaurants and bars, a guide to all these sights as well as free Belgian chocolate. OK, so the last bit's not true. It's sold at the Brussels International Tourism Office (p119) in the Grand Place, and all participating museums. Also consider a voucher booklet, *The Must of Brussels* (€17) which includes 10 vouchers for major city sights, which you select yourself (available from the tourist office and some hotels). Many museums allow free entry from 1pm on the first Wednesday of every month.

MEETING YOUR WATERLOO

On of the most famous battlefields in the world, Waterloo lies 18km south of Brussels and is an easy day trip – although best done with your own vehicle. The site where Napoleon's attempts to control Europe and came to an end once and for all (hence the term 'meeting your Waterloo') requires a vivid imagination or a good reference book to get the most from your visit. On arrival head straight to the **tourist office** (☎ 02 352 09 10 ✉ Chaussée de Bruxelles 218 ☼ 9.30am-6.30pm Apr-Sep, 10.30am-5pm Oct-Mar).

☼ 10am-noon & 1-5pm Sat & Sun, call first Ⓜ Maelbeek

Musée Constantin Meunier (6, C3)
Constantin Meunier was a chronicler of the working class, producing bleak but moving paintings and sculptures depicting people bearing immense burdens. ☎ 02 648 44 49, 02 508 32 11 ✉ Rue de l'Abbaye 59, Ixelles Ⓔ free ☼ call first, weekends only on request or during special exhibitions Ⓜ Louise, then tram 93 or 94

Musée David et Alice van Buuren
This fabulous Art Deco museum, the former home of Dutch banker Van Buuren,

Musée du Costume et de la Dentelle

is now home to an eclectic collection of 15th- to 20th-century art, with work by Pieter Bruegel the Elder, Vincent van Gogh, James Ensor and Rik Wouters, and a wonderful 1.5-hectare garden with maze. ☎ 02 343 48 51 ✉ Ave Léo Errera 41, St-Gilles Ⓔ museum & garden €10/free/5; garden €5/free/2.50 ☼ museum & garden 2-5.30pm Wed-Mon 🚌 90 to Rond-Point Winston Churchill

Musée de la Ville de Bruxelles (4, D5)
The museum of the city in the splendid neo-Gothic Maison du Roi evokes Brussels' past through myriad paintings, models, sculptures, books, historical documents, and… a Manneken Pis (p22) costume exhibition. ☎ 02 279 43 50 ✉ Grand Place, Lower Town Ⓔ €3/free/2.50 ☼ 10am-5pm Tue-Fri, 10am-1pm Sat & Sun Ⓜ De Brouckère 🚌 Bourse

Musée du Cinéma (3, E4)
This small museum on the history of cinema and film-making displays old movie cameras and projection equipment and screens classic, art house and silent films. ☎ 02 507 83 70 ✉ BOZAR/Palais des Beaux-Arts, Rue Baron Horta 9 Ⓔ museum

Atomium (opposite)

free, movie admission €2 ☼ 10am-5pm Tue-Fri, plus film screenings Ⓜ Parc

Musée du Costume et de la Dentelle (4, D6)
One for fans of fashion and lace, this small museum changes its exhibition annually, displaying everyday dress, accessories, lace and embroidery from the 18th to 20th century. ☎ 02 279 44 50 ✉ Rue de la Violette 12 Ⓔ €3 ☼ 10am-12.30pm & 1-5pm Mon, Tue & Thu, 2-5pm Sat & Sun

Musée René Magritte
Surrealist artist René Magritte lived in this modest home from 1930 for 24 years painting over 800 pieces here

and hosting surrealists such as Paul Eluard. Meticulously restored, it has plenty of photos and papers for you to peruse, but only a few paintings.

☎ 02 428 26 26 ✉ Rue Esseghem 135, Jette € €7/6/6 🕑 10am-6pm Wed-Sun Ⓜ Belgica/ Bockstael, then tram 19

NOTABLE BUILDINGS & MONUMENTS

Arcade du Cinquantenaire

Built in 1905 to celebrate Belgium's 50th anniversary of independence in 1880, the monumental arch in the Parc du Cinquantenaire, with its sculpture of a chariot pulled by horses, is spectacular, especially at dusk.

✉ Parc du Cinquantenaire, EU Area Ⓜ Mérode ♿ good

Atomium

This funky steel replica of an iron crystal molecule – magnified 165 billion times to its height of 102m – was built for the 1958 World Fair. Its nine large spheres play host to displays on the history and recent renovation of the Atomium, an exhibition of Jean-Luc Moerman's crazy 'pictorial universe' (imagine kaleidoscopic graffiti, tattoos, decorative cars and furniture etc) until 2007, a restaurant and bar, and from September 2006 a kid's space.

☎ 02 475 47 72 ✉ Square de l'Atomium, Laeken € €9/3/6 🕑 10am-6pm Ⓜ Heysel

Bourse (4, C4)

The grand neoclassical Belgian Stock Exchange building was constructed in 1873 according to architect Léon-Pierre Suys' plans with Auguste Rodin adding some of the sculptures that can be seen on the southwestern façade.

✉ Place de la Bourse, Lower Town Ⓜ De Brouckère 🚋 Bourse

Colonne du Congrès (3, E3)

This striking 50m-high Joseph Poelaert–designed column with wonderful statuary including two majestic lions at its base, and Leopold I at its top, was erected in 1850. The 'eternal' flame burns in memory of Belgians killed in both world wars.

✉ Place du Congrès, Upper Town Ⓜ Botanique ♿ fair

European Parliament

The incredibly ugly and already dated European Parliament building can be toured twice daily when parliament is not sitting, although much of a visit is spent in the empty hemicycle (debating chamber).

☎ 02 284 20 05 ✉ Rue Wiertz 60, EU Area € tours free 🕑 information centre 9am-5.15pm Mon-Fri; tours 10am & 3pm Mon-Thu Ⓜ Maelbeek ♿ excellent

Hôtel de Ville (4, D5)

The splendid 96m-high spire of this wonderful Gothic building is topped by a golden weather vane in the shape of St-Michel, one of Brussels' patron saints. Beautifully lit at night, it will become a reference point for you during your stay. Tours take in the beautiful interiors, with portraits, decorative arts and, most notably, 15th-century Flemish tapestries.

☎ 02 548 04 45 ✉ Grand Place, Lower Town € tours €3 🕑 tours 3.15pm Tue & Wed year-round, 10.45am & 12.15pm Sun Apr-Sep Ⓜ De Brouckère 🚋 Bourse ♿ good

Maison de la Bellone (4, A2)

Taking its name from Bellona, the goddess of war, whose statue is above the main entrance, the Maison de la Bellone is most visited by tourists wanting to admire its stunning 17th-century façade, protected from the weather under a glass canopy, but it's also home to the **Maison du Spectacle**, a dramatic performing arts centre.

☎ 02 513 33 33 ✉ Rue de Flandre 46, Lower Town 🕑 12pm-5pm Tue-Fri Ⓜ Ste-Catherine ♿ fair

Hôtel de Ville

Wee Manneken Pis

Manneken Pis (4, C6)
Tourists flock to this underwhelming 30cm-high statuette of a naked boy pissing in the street. It's apparently ironic, and meant to capture the city's rebellious spirit – we think it just reflects everyday habits in the city.
✉ cnr Rue de l'Étuve & Rue du Chêne, Lower Town Ⓜ Gare Centrale 🚋 Bourse ♿ good

Palais de Justice (3, C6)
The architect of the imposing edifice, Joseph Poelaert, died before it was completed. The law house took 17 years to be finished and is worth a look for its enormous interior forecourt and 100m-high dome. Next to it, Place Poelaert, has interesting views over the Lower Town rooftops and a large elevator takes people to the Marolles below.
☎ 02 508 61 11 ✉ Place Poelaert, Upper Town € free ⏰ 8.30am-5pm Mon-Fri Ⓜ Louise ♿ good

Palais Royal (3, E5)
Built on the site of ancient Coudenberg Palace, the Palais Royal can be toured one month each year to admire its impressive Throne Room, rococo drawing rooms, and lavish Hall of Mirrors.
☎ 02 551 20 20 ✉ Place des Palais, Upper Town € free ⏰ 10.30am-4.30pm Tue-Sun Jul-Aug Ⓜ Parc ♿ excellent

Porte de Hal
The sole surviving gateway out of the seven that were part of the city's second perimeter wall in the 14th century, and once a prison, it now houses temporary historical exhibitions.
✉ Blvd du Midi, St-Gilles Ⓜ Porte de Hal ♿ good

Tour d'Angle (3, D4)
The Tour d'Angle (Corner Tower) is one of 50 defensive towers that reared up along the original city wall's 4km length that encircled the city in the 12th century.
✉ Blvd de l'Empereur, Upper Town Ⓜ Gare Centrale ♿ good

CHURCHES & CATHEDRALS

Église Notre Dame de la Chapelle (3, C5)
A fascinating blend of Romanesque and Gothic styles, the city's oldest church was completed in the 13th century. The resting place of Pieter Bruegel the Elder, buried here in 1569 is what most come to see.
☎ 02 512 07 37 ✉ Rue des Ursulines 4, Marolles Ⓜ Gare Centrale 🚋 Anneessens

Palais Royal in twilight

Église Notre Dame du Sablon (3, D5)

Built by a guild of crossbow enthusiasts at the start of the 14th century, this late-Gothic church is notable for its size, baroque chapels, sculpted pulpit and stained-glass windows.

☎ 02 511 57 41 ✉ Rue de la Régence 3b, Sablon Ⓜ Porte de Namur ♿ fair

Église St-Jacques sur Coudenberg (3, E5)

This neoclassical church, dating from 1785, contains some impressive Jan Portaels paintings, a Laurent Delvaux statue and a striking 19th-century Spanish Madonna.

☎ 02 511 78 36 ✉ Place Royale, Upper Town ⏰ 1-6pm Tue-Sat, 9am-6pm Sun Ⓜ Trône

PARKS & GARDENS

Forêt de Soignes

The forest parks of the **Bois de la Cambre** (☎ 02 629 34 11; Ixelles; tram 93 &

JEAN-BERNARD CARILLET

Parc de Laeken

JEAN-BERNARD CARILLET

Watching the world go by in Parc de Bruxelles

94; ♿ fair) and the larger Forêt de Soignes in the southeast of Brussels with their peaceful ponds provide lovely tranquil escapes from the city. The meditative 12th-century monastery, Abbaye de la Cambre, and Rouge Cloître, a 14th-century abbey, make the setting very picturesque.

✉ Auderghem ⏰ 2-6pm Tue-Sun May-Oct, 2-5pm Tue-Sun Nov-Apr Ⓜ Herrmann-Debroux 🚌 95 from Bourse

Parc de Bruxelles (3, E4)

Handy to the Mont des Arts (the area where most of the city's finest museums are located), Brussels' most popular park, with wonderful statuary, an old bandstand, (empty) fountain ponds and kiosks, makes an ideal resting spot in between sights.

✉ Upper Town Ⓜ Parc ♿ good

Parc de Laeken

Near the Atomium (p21), Mini-Europe (p25) and the Château Royal, this park of rolling ground and groves of trees is great for picnics and games of sport.

✉ Laeken Ⓜ Heysel ♿ fair

Parc Léopold

This hilly park behind the European Parliament has a small lake, but apart from local kids playing basketball and the odd person walking a dog, it's used more as a thoroughfare than a place to relax.

✉ EU Area Ⓜ Maelbeek ♿ fair

Square Marie-Louise

'Square' Marie-Louise is actually a large tree-lined duck pond bordered by slim strips of green, in a neighbourhood smattered with Art Nouveaux architecture (p24). Ave Palmerston connects it to **Square Ambroix**, another Brussels park filled with empty fountain-ponds and some beautiful statuary, separating the characterless expat EU area from the more colourful Muslim neighbourhood of Schaerbeek.

✉ EU Area Ⓜ Schuman or Maelbeek

PLACES & STREETS

Place des Martyrs (4, F2)

The 467 patriots who died during the 1830 Belgian revolt against the Dutch lie under the monument in the

ART NOUVEAU

Brussels was at the cutting edge of the new style of architecture and decoration known as Art Nouveau that started in the 1880s and flourished at the turn of the 20th century. Organic, sinuous and feminine, using material such as wrought iron, glass, timbers and marble, the Art Nouveau movement lasted up until WWI. While many buildings haven't survived and many have been altered, there are still some stunning examples worth checking out in the city:

- Musée Horta (p17)
- Musée des Instruments de Musique (p16) — the Old England building
- De Ultieme Hallucinatie (p35)
- Falstaff (p44)
- Centre Belge de la Bande Dessinée (p14)

LEANNE LOGAN

centre of this pretty cobblestone square lined with a few bookshops.
⊠ Lower Town
Ⓜ De Brouckère

Place du Grand Sablon
(3, D5)
Place du Grand Sablon is home to a weekend connoisseurs antique market by beautiful Gothic Église Notre

MARTIN MOOS

Place du Grand Sablon

Dame du Sablon (p23), but unfortunately has a car park at its centre. Across busy Rue de la Régence is **Place du Petit Sablon**, a delightful formal garden planted in 1890 and fenced in by a balustrade of 48 bronze statues, each representing a medieval guild.
⊠ Upper Town Ⓜ Porte de Namur ♿ fair

Place Royale (3, E4)
This busy roundabout – with a statue of 11th-century crusader Godfroide de Bouillon at its centre – is surrounded by majestic neoclassical buildings, including the Musées Royaux des Beaux-Arts de Belgique (p15) and Musée des Instruments de Musique (p16). This whole area, concentrated with some of the city's best museums, is known as the Mont des Arts. There's a stunning view of the grand Palais de

Justice (p22) at the end of Rue de la Régence.
⊠ Place Royale, Upper Town Ⓜ Parc ♿ good

Rue des Bouchers (4, E4)
Now a busy lane of cheap tourist restaurants, this cobblestone street was once home to the city's butchers, hence its name (Butchers' Street). Worth a walk in the evening for the bustle and neon lights, but avoid eating here unless you have to.
⊠ Lower Town Ⓜ De Brouckère ♿ fair

QUIRKY BRUSSELS

Jeanneke Pis (4, E4)
Confirming that the sequels never do as well as the original, the lonely sister to Manneken Pis, erected some 20-odd years ago, doesn't seem to do much urinating,

locked behind bars as she is in an alley off Rue des Bouchers with a stagnant basin of water at her feet.

✉ Impasse de la Fidélité, Lower Town Ⓜ De Brouckère Ⓡ Bourse ♿ good

Zinneke Pis (4, A4)
The kooky canine companion to the pissing preteens is generally met with a smile and while the statue of a dog watering a post apparently symbolises Brussels' irreverent spirit, if our canine friend was performing another 'doggily' function, that would better represent what you'll actually see on the ground... ✉ Rue Charles Buls, Lower Town Ⓜ De Brouckère Ⓡ Bourse ♿ good

BRUSSELS FOR CHILDREN

Bruparck
This sprawling amusement park is home to Mini-Europe, with 300 miniature reproductions of iconic European sites; Océade, a water park; a planetarium; the Kinepolis cinemas; and eateries at the Village.
☎ 02 474 83 77 🖳 www .bruparck.com in Dutch & French ✉ Blvd du Centenaire 20, Laeken € various admission prices, check website for details or visit tourist office ☉ hours vary, check website Ⓜ Heysel ♿ good

Muséum des Sciences Naturelles de Belgique
Despite being housed in a drab '70s-style building, this old-fashioned museum has plenty of changing thematic,

interactive exhibitions to amuse and educate the kids, with recent exhibitions – Simply Mussels and the Heart at Work – proving popular.
☎ 02 627 42 38 ✉ Rue Vautier 29, EU Area € permanent collection €4/1.50/3, incl temporary exhibitions €7/4.50/6 ☉ 9.30am-4.45pm Tue-Fri, 10am-6pm Sat & Sun Ⓜ Maelbeek ♿ good

Scientastic Museum
(4, C4)
This subterranean low-tech science museum under the Bourse gives kids the chance to experience 80 hands-on science experiments and 1001 astonishing effects of science that put all senses to the test.
☎ 02 732 13 36 ✉ Bourse

station, Lower Town € €6.10/4.60 ☉ 12.30-2pm Mon-Fri, 2-5.30pm Sat, Sun & school holidays Ⓜ De Brouckère Ⓡ Bourse

Théâtre Royal de Toone
(4, E5)
This pokey theatre's wood-and-papier-mâché marionettes have been performing productions of Faust and Hamlet since 1830, thanks to puppet pioneer Antoine ('Toone') Gente and his seven generations of descendants.
☎ 02 511 71 37 🖳 www .toone.be ✉ Impasse Schuddeveld 6 (Petite Rue des Bouchers 21), Lower Town € €10/7 ☉ shows 8.30pm Wed-Sat Feb-Dec, occasional matinees, call first Ⓜ Gare Centrale ♿ good

Marionettes at play at Théâtre Royal de Toone.

Belgians aren't fanatical about shopping in the way that many Europeans are, yet they still have an appreciation for fine things, love their fabulous Belgian fashion and are familiar with quality brands.

Belgians are window-shoppers – shopping is generally something they do leisurely on their way to somewhere else, something that fits into a Saturday that may be filled with a long lunch out, a visit to an art gallery and a stroll in the park.

And after they've had their fill of shopping, they will move on to somewhere else – purchases in hand – to have a drink at, say, a St-Géry bar, or perhaps catch a bit of 'after-shopping jazz' at swish jazz bar L'Archiduc (p45). Belgium has given birth to its fair share of jazz legends, and Belgians are big jazz fans, as well as connoisseurs of classical music, so it's no surprise their music stores are always full. And while they may not be known for their literature, they're avid readers and bookshops tend to be packed, particularly on weekends.

Tourists in Belgian love to buy handmade Belgium lace, gourmet chocolates and fine Belgian beers, but Belgian fashion, especially the idiosyncratic Antwerp designs (such as of the Antwerp 6), are great buys. You'll find beautifully made shoes, handbags, hats and jewellery difficult to find else-

Bric-a-brac in Marolles

where. Belgium has a large Congolese population, so for something different, check out the African crafts in Brussels' Matongé and Marolles areas. Belgians are also mad about bric-a-brac, antiques and 20th-century design objects, and you'll find unique souvenirs in shops and markets in the Sablon and Rue Blaes.

While shopping hours in Brussels' centre are generally from 10am to 6pm Monday to Saturday, this can give or take by half an hour. Some shops may open later if they're closing later and, if they stay open Sunday, close one other day of the week. The year's main *soldes* (sales) are in January and July.

Foreign visitors who aren't EU residents can reclaim the tax paid on purchases, provided they spend a minimum of €125 in a shop with a 'Tax Free Shopping' sign, get a tax refund cheque when paying (very important!) and get the cheque stamped by customs when departing (they must exit the EU within three months of the purchase).

HOT SHOPPING AREAS

- Rue Antoine Dansaert, St-Géry (4, A2) – *the* place to shop for Belgian fashion at its best, from established labels to small independent designers, jewellery, shoes and accessories
- Rue des Chartreux, St-Géry (4, A4) – alternative fashion, art galleries and interior-design objects
- Place Ste-Catherine (4, B2) – fishmongers, delicatessens, coffee roasters, fine foods, herbalists, Asian and Latin American supermarkets and mushroom specialists
- Blvd Anspach and Rue des Pierres (4, B5 & C5) – endless comic-book shops, second-hand bookstores, music shops and vintage clothing
- Galeries Royales St-Hubert and around Grand Place (4, E4 & D5) – elegant arcade shopping, fine books and classical music, chocolates, beer, lace, Belgian regional products, leather goods and souvenirs
- Rue Neuve (4, E2) – a pedestrian strip with global high street brands and City 2 shopping mall
- Ave Louise and Blvd Waterloo (4, D6) – exclusive international luxury brands
- Place du Grand Sablon (3, D5) – antiques and designer brands
- Chaussée de Wavre, Matongé (3, F6) – African textiles and clothing, Galerie d'Ixelles, music, hair extensions and wigs
- Rue Blaes, Marolles (3, C5) – *brocante* (bric-a-brac), antiques, 20th-century design objects, art galleries and African crafts

ARCADES & SHOPPING CENTRES

City 2 (3, E2)
The main reason you might want to visit this shopping mall is for every traveller's friend, FNAC, with its offerings of guide books, maps, memory cards, iPod accessories, camera and video gear, CDs and DVDs (including a good Belgian selection) and English-language books. You'll also find the usual franchises you see around the world these days, from the Body Shop to Zara.
☎ 02 211 40 60 ✉ Rue Neuve 123, Lower Town ◷ 10am-7pm Ⓜ Rogier

Galerie Agora (4, E6)
This lively arcade is worth a look for its hundred-plus shops. While some sell street wear, hippy gear and disco threads, most shops sell leather – jackets, coats, belts and bags. Although a lot of the stuff is dated in style, other pieces are classics, and some of the retro-looking jackets are just too cool.
☎ 02 513 65 72 ✉ Rue des Eperonniers, Lower Town Ⓜ Gare Centrale

Galeries Louise (3, D6)
This conservative upmarket mall offers a few good boutiques and some interesting jewellery, although much of it is overpriced. It's probably most interesting for people-watching if high-society spending interests you.
✉ Ave Louise, Ixelles ◷ 6.30am-9.30pm Mon-Sat, 9am-9pm Sun Ⓜ Louise

Sip a coffee in Galeries Royales St-Hubert (p28)

IAN TAKEAWAYS

- Chocolate (p10) – look for Leonidas, Neuhaus, Godiva, Wittamer, Galler and Pierre Marcolini
- Beer (p9) – hundreds to choose from, so opt for a 'Belgian Tour' gift box if you can't decide!
- Lace (p33) – buy it while it's back in fashion but make sure it's handmade
- Belgian comics (p32) – try the Centre Belge de la Bande Dessinée (p14) bookshop or Brüsel for something different
- Fashion (below) – Christa Reniers jewellery or a Christophe Coppens hat won't send the baggage allowance over

Christophe Coppens

Galeries Royales St-Hubert (4, E4)

Europe's oldest and the city's most elegant shopping arcade consists of three interconnected glass-vaulted promenades – Galerie de la Reine, Galerie du Roi and Galerie des Princes – which are home to some wonderful stores: fine chocolate shops, leather goods, designer boutiques, bookshops and design stores.

✉ entry at Rue du Marché aux Herbes & at Rue de l'Écuyer, Lower Town
Ⓜ Gare Centrale

Delvaux

CLOTHING & ACCESSORIES

Bouvy (3, D6)

The collections at Bouvy's women's store on Ave Louise (specialising in mainly Italian labels such as Armani, Cerutti, Rivamonti and Louisa Cerrano) are very chic and their windows fab. The adjoining men's store (entered from Ave de la Toison d'Or) is dull in comparison.

☎ 02 513 07 48 ✉ Ave Louise 4, Ixelles Ⓨ 11am-6.30pm Mon, 10am-6.30pm Tue-Sat Ⓜ Louise

Christa Reniers (4, B3)

Once the arresting window displays of Christa Reniers, Belgium's best jewellery designer, lure you in to the store, you'll have a hard time deciding between her splendid contemporary jewellery (often crafted with sterling silver into organic forms embellished with gems) and her bold ceramics.

☎ 02 510 06 60 ✉ Rue Antoine Dansaert 29, Lower Town Ⓨ 10.30am-1pm & 2-6.30pm Mon-Sat Ⓜ Ste-Catherine Ⓡ Bourse

Christophe Coppens (4, A2)

A former theatre designer, Coppens is one of Europe's most successful milliners, hand-crafting the kind of fine hats you see on the catwalks (and made cool on the heads of pop singers and movie stars), along with more extravagant styles worn to ritzy weddings and racing carnivals.

☎ 02 512 77 97 ✉ Rue Léon Lepage 2, Lower Town Ⓨ 11am-6pm Tue-Sat Ⓜ Ste-Catherine

Delvaux (4, E5)

Europe's oldest leather goods house, Delvaux started in Brussels 175 years ago and is the bag of choice for Belgium's royal women. Though expensive, they're stylish, strong and beautifully handcrafted, and will last forever.

☎ 02 512 71 98 ✉ Galerie de la Reine 31, Lower Town Ⓨ 10am-6.30pm Mon-Sat Ⓜ Gare Centrale

Hatshoe (4, A2)

This elegant Art Deco store is the spot to hit if you're after unique, high-quality hats

JEAN-BERNARD CARILLET

and shoes by famous Belgian designers such as Dries Van Noten and Véronique Branquinho, and French brands such as Costume National, Robert Clergerie and Muxart.
☎ 02 512 41 52
✉ Rue Antoine Dansaert 89, Lower Town ⏲ 10.30am-6.30pm Tue-Sat, 12.30-6.30pm Mon Ⓜ Ste-Catherine Ⓡ Bourse

IdeB Lifestore (3, D6)
This fabulous designer department store specialises in men's and women's prêt-a-porter collections, lingerie, jewellery and accessories, from such designers as Barbara Bui, Paul Smith and Christian Lacroix, while their own label, IdeB, specialises in mix-and-match pieces in myriad colours. Apart from clothes, the store also offers cosmetics, a home interiors section and a stylish bar and restaurant.
☎ 02 289 11 10
✉ Blvd de Waterloo 49, Upper Town ⏲ 10.30am-7pm Tue-Fri, 11am-7pm Sat, 2-7pm Mon Ⓜ Louise

Mademoiselle Jean (3, C3)
Inspired by the past, Aurore Jean's hand-made contemporary women's range has a preloved vintage look and feel to it. Many of her feminine pieces look like lingerie (very sexy) with lace and ribbons embellishing them, and she also creates beautiful corsets.
☎ 02 513 50 69
✉ Rue Antoine Dansaert 100, Lower Town
⏲ 11am-6.30pm Tue-Sat
Ⓜ Ste-Catherine Ⓡ Bourse

Martin Margiela (4, A1)
After graduating from the fashion department of Antwerp's Academy of Fine Arts in the mid '80s, Margiela worked for Jean Paul Gaultier for a few years before establishing his own label, and Gaultier's influence – a deconstructed look, visible stitching, asymmetrical hems, lots of black – is also present in Margiela's style. Buzz to enter his flagship Brussels store.
☎ 02 223 75 20
✉ Rue Léon Lepage, Lower Town ⏲ 11am-7pm Mon-Sat Ⓜ Ste-Catherine Ⓡ Bourse

Rue Blanche (4, B3)
This is probably the closest thing that Rue Antoine Dansaert has to a high street store. This stylish shop (with arty window displays) established by Belgian designers Marie Chantal Regout and Patrick Van Heurck specialises in colourful, fun, classic pieces that easily mix and match, and coordinate well with their vibrant accessories. We love the whole vibe of the store!
☎ 02 512 03 14 ✉ Rue Antoine Dansaert 35-39, Lower Town ⏲ 11am-6.30pm Mon-Sat Ⓜ Ste-Catherine Ⓡ Bourse

Shampoo & Conditioner (4, A4)
Stunning Aude de Wolf and Vanessa Vukicevic's range is a return to a feminine 1940s to '50s fashion with fitted shirts, pencil skirts, and body-hugging uniform-style frocks – even when they do the military look it's chic and sexy. The made-to-measure garments are created in their atelier at the back of the pretty store.
☎ 02 511 07 77
✉ Rue des Chartreux 18, Lower Town ⏲ 10am-6pm Mon-Sat Ⓜ Ste-Catherine Ⓡ Bourse

Stijl (4, A2)
For over 20 years owner Sonja Noël has promoted Belgian fashion, stocking all the best labels, helped develop Rue Antoine Dansaert into a fashion centre, and continues to support young designers like Cathy Pill whose collection she stocks. This fresh talent wowed Paris in 2005 with a collection of fabulous frocks printed with graphics inspired by Art Nouveau architecture.
☎ 02 512 03 13 ✉ Rue Antoine Dansaert 74, Lower Town ⏲ 10.30am-6.30pm Mon-Sat Ⓜ Ste-Catherine Ⓡ Bourse

JEAN-BERNARD CARILLET

Leather goods fit for royalty at Delvaux (opposite)

BROCANTE, ANTIQUES & DESIGN

Broc Ant Art (3, C5)

On a street full of *brocante* (bric-a-brac) dealers, this is one of the most reliably interesting with myriad curios and collectables, from old board games in kitsch packaging to groovy airline bags, 1950s clocks, retro ceramics and coloured glass vases.
☎ 02 511 43 04
✉ Rue Blaes 59, Marolles
🕑 10am-6pm Mon-Fri, 10am-3pm Sat Ⓜ Porte de Hal

Espace Bizarre (4, B4)

In addition to stocking one of the most comprehensive selections of quality contemporary furniture from Belgian and international designers, Espace Bizarre also has smaller design products that travel better than a Birdman oak coffee table, as wonderful as they may be, such as Pia Wallen felt slippers from Sweden or a bright Saskia Marcotti boot bag from Belgium.
☎ 02 514 52 56
✉ Rue des Chartreux 17-19, Ste-Catherine 🕑 10am 7pm Mon-Sat Ⓜ Ste-Catherine
🚇 Bourse

Naughty statues in the Sablon Antiques Center
JEAN-BERNARD CARILLET

Sablon Antiques Center (3, D5)

There are scores of antique stores on the Place du Grand Sablon and its surrounding streets, but here you have a couple of dozen dealers in a 'one-stop shop' on the Sablon itself, selling everything from ceramics and jewellery to furniture and fine art.
☎ 02 502 19 29 🖥 www .antiquessablon.com
✉ Place du Grand Sablon 39, Sablon 🕑 10am-6pm Ⓜ Porte de Namur

MUSIC & BOOKS

Bozarshop (3, E4)

As you'd expect from this fabulous cultural and exhibition-space-cum-performing-arts-centre, it has an excellent bookshop with glossy books and texts on artists, fine arts, architecture, culture and literature, as well as an eclectic collection of CDs, art-themed gifts and the odd bestseller.
☎ 02 507 83 33 ✉ BOZAR/ Palais des Beaux-Arts, Rue Ravenstein 23, Upper Town
🕑 10am-6pm Tue-Sun
Ⓜ Parc

Excellence (4, C4)

One for the cineastes – this has to be one of the best DVD stores in the world, with an enormous selection of art house, independent, classic and foreign films from all over the globe, including works by Belgian filmmakers, such as Chantal Ackerman and the Dardenne brothers. Just make sure the subtitles are in your language of choice.
☎ 02 502 84 68 ✉ Blvd Anspach 94-96, Lower Town
🕑 10am-6pm Ⓜ De Brouckère 🚇 Bourse

BELGIANS AND THE BIG SCREEN

Belgian movie directors have achieved much success internationally. The following films received wide release, and tell us more about Belgians through their direction rather than their content:

- *Golden Eighties* (1986) – Chantal Ackerman
- *Toto the Hero* (1991, Cannes Caméra d'Or winner) – Jaco Van Dormael
- *Man Bites Dog* (1992) – Rémy Belvaux, André Bonzel and Benoît Poelvoorde
- *Antonia's Line* (1995, Best Foreign Film Oscar winner) – Marleen Gorris
- *The Child* (2005, Cannes Palmes d'Or winner) – Jean-Pierre and Luc Dardenne

BELGIUM READS

Belgians do more reading than they do writing, but here's a mixed bag of reads set in Belgium, by Belgians and about Belgium:

- *Brüsel* (comic) – Benoit Peeters (author) & François Schuiten (artist)
- *The Sorrow of Belgium* – Hugo Claus
- *The Character of Rain* – Amélie Nothomb
- *Falling* – Anne Provoost
- *Antwerp* – Nicholas Royle
- *The King Incorporated: Leopold the Second and the Congo* – Neal Ascherson
- *The Art of Being Belgian* – Richard Hill
- *Great Beers of Belgium* – Michael Jackson
- *Everybody Eats Well in Belgium Cookbook* – Ruth Van Waerebeek

Bozarshop (opposite)

Goupil-O-Phone (4, B5)

The collection is so diverse and the prices so low at this largely second-hand music emporium that it's hard to leave without buying something. Stocking vinyl, CDs and DVDs, with a decent selection of limited editions, there's also new stock if you can't find anything at preloved prices.
☎ 02 511 00 74 ✉ Blvd Anspach 101, Lower Town 🕑 10.30am-7pm Ⓜ De Brouckère 🚋 Bourse

La Boîte à Musique (3, E4)

With a comprehensive classical-music and opera CD and DVD collection that many consider to be the best in Europe, it's impossible to leave here without finding what you want. If you don't know what you want, consult the experts, they're happy to help. It's handily placed near the Musée des Instruments de Musique (p16).
☎ 02 513 09 65 ✉ Coudenberg 74, Upper Town 🕑 9.30am-4pm Mon-Sat Ⓜ Parc

Le Bonheur (3, B2)

On an increasingly interesting street, in an immigrant neighbourhood with Bollywood tape shops and Middle Eastern grocery stores, Le Bonheur has an eclectic range of short films, video art and animation on DVD, interesting CDs from experimental electronica to world music, graphic-design books and sometimes DJs. Head across to Walvis (p46) for a drink when you're done browsing.
☎ 02 511 64 14 ✉ Rue Antoine Dansaert 196

🕑 11am-7pm Mon-Sat Ⓜ Ste-Catherine

Librairie des Galeries (4, E4)

This wonderful bookshop in the elegant Galerie du Roi has some beautiful coffee table books on Belgium, its rich history, art and architecture, as well as travel guides, along with fabulous books on fine arts, performing arts and artists in general, many of which are in English.
☎ 02 511 24 12 ✉ Galerie du Roi 2, Lower Town 🕑 10am-6.30pm Tue-Sat, 1.30-6.30pm Sun & Mon Ⓜ Gare Centrale

Spend an afternoon browsing Pêle-Mêle (p32)

SOUNDS OF THE CITY

Brussels can provide some eclectic soundtracks for your visit and to remember your visit after you get home. Here's a brief selection:
- Django Reinhardt, *The Best of Django Reinhardt* – a great starting point for discovering this brilliant guitarist, composer and jazz icon
- Jacques Brel, *Brel Vol. 1 (Master Serie)* – a fine introduction to this legendary singer and songwriter, who never lost his connection to Belgium
- Plastic Bertrand, *Plastic Bertrand* – a 'Best of' including mega-hit 'Ça Plane Pour Moi'
- Dirty Dancing, *Histoire d'Amour* – compilation from Mirano's Dirty Dancing (p46) night
- Hooverphonic, *Blue Wonder Powder Milk* – the band's woozy mix of beats, jazzy overtones and sound snippets is perfect for an overcast Belgian day

Pêle-Mêle (3, C4)
Primarily a second-hand bookshop with enormous rooms of fiction and non-fiction in French, Dutch and English, there's also a room at the back with second-hand Belgian and French comics and Japanese manga, as well a room full of vinyl and CDs. With books going for €1, as you'd expect, it's madness on weekends.
☎ 02 548 78 00 ✉ Blvd Maurice Lemonnier 55, Lower Town ⌚ 10am-6.30pm Mon-Sat Ⓜ De Brouckère Ⓡ Anneessens

COMICS

Brüsel (4, C4)
This comic-strip store, on a street full of them, is popular for its great range of Belgian favourites and international comics, including the extraordinarily popular Japanese manga, along with a range of whacky comic character figures. We love their illustrative 'How to Ruin Your Life, Draw Cartoons, and Doom Yourself!' poster.
☎ 02 502 35 52 ✉ Blvd Anspach 100, Lower Town ⌚ 10.30am-6.30pm Mon-Sat, noon-6.30pm Sun Ⓜ De Brouckère Ⓡ Bourse

La Boutique Tintin (4, E5)
Tourists cram this store to take home the much-coveted comic books about traveller-reporter Tintin's global adventures that seem to be igniting imaginations increasingly more these days. You'll discover English translations, wonderful Tintin posters, toys, trinkets and T-shirts.
☎ 02 514 51 52 ✉ Rue de la Colline 13, Lower Town ⌚ 10am-6pm Mon-Sat, 11am-5pm Sun Ⓜ Gare Centrale Ⓡ Bourse

FOR CHILDREN

Grasshopper (4, D4)
This enormous two-storey toy shop has everything a child could possibly covet, from classics such as cuddly bears, kaleidoscopes and colourful old-fashioned wooden toys to challenging educational toys and games that are ideal for keeping them occupied while travelling.
☎ 02 511 96 22 ✉ Rue du Marché aux Herbes 39, Lower Town ⌚ 10.30am-6.30pm Mon-Sat Ⓜ Gare Centrale Ⓡ Bourse

Kat en Muis (4, A3)
This delightful kids clothes store stocks some wonderful whimsical fashion for little boys and girls – when we last looked, the window glowed with vibrant coats and funky boots, summery Hawaiian printed skirts and rainbow-coloured cardigans, and zany printed shirts with big baggy shorts.

Tintin on the moon at La Boutique Tintin

☎ 02 514 32 34 ✉ Rue
Antoine Dansaert 34,
Ste-Catherine ⏲ 10.30am-
6.30pm Mon-Sat
Ⓜ Ste-Catherine

FOOD & DRINK

Champigros (4, B3)
On a street that was once
known by locals as Rue des
Champignons, or Mushroom
Street, this family-run business, operating since 1950,
is the last of the specialist
mushroom suppliers. While
they mainly sell wonderful
fresh seasonal mushrooms
to locals and the very best
restaurants around town,
there are jars of truffles and
tapenades for travellers to
take home.
☎ 02 511 74 98 ✉ Rue
Melsens 22, Lower Town
⏲ 7.30am-5pm Tue-Sat
Ⓜ Ste-Catherine

A M Sweet (4, B4)
This delightful sweet shop
sells Belgian chocolates,
biscuits and confectionary
in charming packaging, and
Freres Mariage teas from
Paris – they all make great

De Biertempel

Intricate lace at Manufacture Belge de Dentelles

gifts! – as well as home-
made cakes, pies and pastries
to take back to the hotel or
enjoy in their tiny tearoom.
☎ 02 513 51 31 ✉ Rue
des Chartreux 4, Lower Town
⏲ 8.30am-7pm Mon-Sat
Ⓜ Ste-Catherine Ⓤ Bourse

BELGIAN SPECIALTIES

De Biertempel (4, E5)
If you can find a time to
visit the store when it's not
crowded with tourists taking
home beer souvenirs, then
you'll find over 450 beers
here, gift sets with glasses,
kitsch beer trays and the
obligatory T-shirts and bottle
openers.
☎ 02 502 19 06 ✉ Rue du
Marché aux Herbes 56, Lower
Town ⏲ 9.30am-7pm
Ⓜ De Brouckère Ⓤ Bourse

Manufacture Belge de Dentelles (4, E5)
One of Brussels' oldest lace
shops has an expansive range
of hand-made and machine-
made lace, and by looking
at the price you'll be able to
tell which is which. There
are some wonderful intricate
old pieces in addition to
newer items, such as boxed

handkerchiefs, which make
lovely gifts for grandma.
☎ 02 511 44 77 ✉ Galerie
de la Reine 6-8, Lower Town
⏲ 9.30am-6pm Mon-Sat
Ⓜ Gare Centrale Ⓤ Bourse

Neuhaus (4, E5)
In the elegant Galeries
Royales St-Hubert, Neuhaus
has the most mouth-
watering window displays
and the fine chocolates meet
expectations. They also have
great souvenir gift boxes that
travel well.
☎ 02 512 63 59 🖥 www
.neuhaus.be ✉ Galerie de
la Reine 25-27, Lower Town
⏲ 10am-8pm Mon-Sat,
11am-7pm Sun Ⓜ Gare
Centrale

Pierre Marcolini (3, D5)
Not only does Pierre Mar-
colini, one of Belgium's
oldest chocolate makers,
have the chicest store, the
most elegant packaging and
the best pralines, but the
chocolates consistently win
awards.
☎ 02 514 12 06 🖥 www
.marcolini.be ✉ Place du
Grand Sablon 39, Sablon
⏲ 10am-7pm Mon-Thu,
10am-8pm Fri, 9am-9pm
Sat, 9am-7pm Sun Ⓜ Porte
de Namur

JEAN-BERNARD CARILLET

DOUG MCKINLAY

Brussels is a good eating city. Bruxellois love dishes that combine the freshest ingredients, flawless preparation, great presentation and convivial surroundings in which to enjoy them. The good news for visitors is that this notion is inherent in Brussels' restaurants from the smallest local bistro serving classic Flemish specialties to the French-flavoured *haute cuisine* establishments. Just as Brussels keeps its traditional cuisine alive, it's also a city that isn't about to give up the tradition of the long lunch. Whether it be for business or pleasure, Bruxellois like to keep the conversation, dishes and wines or beer coming for as long as everyone's willing to stay.

While in the hotels you'll generally be offered some sliced meats, cheese, bread and coffee for breakfast, Bruxellois tend to snack on *maatjes* (herring fillets) or a *sandwich garni* (a filled half-baguette) mid-morning. For lunch you should try some old Belgian favourites such as *moules et frites* (mussels and fries, see p37), *waterzooi* (fish or chicken stew) or *stoemp* (mashed potatoes with cabbage) usually accompanied by some *saucisses* (sausages), and while these dishes might seem heavy, given the weather that Brussels is often saddled with, comfort food is the order of the day! Keep in mind that for lunch, many of Brussels' top restaurants have excellent fixed-price menus that are worth checking out.

For dinner with friends, Bruxellois like to head somewhere more stylish and Brussels obliges by having some fine looking restaurants serving up superb *truffe* (truffle) dishes, fresh oysters and other top-shelf ingredients. Dinner is a great time to check out some of the locals favourites in areas like Ixelles, St-Gilles and Matongé.

Smoking is slowly becoming less common in Belgium's many restaurants, cafés and brasseries, and some establishments have now banned smoking outright. A service charge is almost always included in restaurant bills, but of course you can leave a tip if you feel like it. Note that many menus are written exclusively in French and Flemish – however if the restaurant offers a menu in six languages, it's probably a good idea to move on (see p38).

RICK GERHARTER

ST-JOSSE & SCHAERBEEK

De Ultieme Hallucinatie (3, F1)

Traditional Belgian €€-€€€
This is a gorgeous Art Nouveau (1904) eatery, with a low-lit restaurant and a brasserie at the rear. We generally opt for the brasserie – while it's not as pretty as the restaurant, the less fussy fare is more fun. Try mussels or pastas in the brasserie or a set menu out the front.

☎ 02 217 06 14 🖳 www .ultiemehallucinatie.be ✉ Rue Royale 316 🕒 11am-late Mon-Fri, 4pm-late Sat Ⓜ Botanique

L'Ane Vert (3, F1)

Traditional Belgian €€
This welcoming local brasserie serves up hearty dishes such as *coq au vin* (chicken stew) in its cosy room, and outside when the weather is agreeable. There are some decent vegetarian options on the menu and some good wines and beers on offer.

☎ 02 217 26 17 🖳 www.anevert.be in French ✉ Rue Royale Ste-Marie 11 🕒 noon-midnight Mon-Fri, 5pm-midnight Sat Ⓜ Botanique Ⓥ

Metin (3, F1)

Turkish €
In an atmospheric street (after dark) filled with *pide* places, Metin is the absolute king of Turkish pizzas, so much so that there's a Metin 2 on the same street (at No 83). Try the pizza with just about any topping you can think of, including eggs –

Find out for yourself if Metin is the king of Turkish pizza

JEAN-BERNARD CARILLET

but we love it with Turkish sausage.

☎ 02 217 68 63 ✉ Chaussée de Haecht 94 🕒 11am-11pm Wed-Mon Ⓜ Botanique Ⓥ

GRAND PLACE AREA & ILÔT SACRÉ

Aux Armes de Bruxelles (4, E4)

Traditional Belgian €€€
In a street where dining is a minefield of mussel places, this elegant eatery is where locals come to get treated royally and eat some fantastic seafood. The oysters are the freshest around and for mains try any version of the mussels or fish – the *sole meuniere* (fish with butter and lemon) is excellent.

☎ 02 511 55 50 🖳 www .armesdebruxelles.be ✉ Rue des Bouchers 13 🕒 noon-11pm Tue-Sun Ⓜ De Brouckère 🚇 Bourse

Belga Queen (4, E2)

Modern Belgian €€€-€€€€
The Belga Queen is Brussels' queen of indulgence. Generous opening hours, a fabulous restaurant with an equally fab crowd settled in it, a lustrous *ecailler*

(oyster bar) and a cigar bar leave you no excuses for not visiting at least once. The main menu (split between meat and fish) even has a vegetarian section and low-calorie options for the supermodels.

☎ 02 217 21 87 🖳 www .belgaqueen.be ✉ Rue du Fossé aux Loups 32 🕒 kitchen noon-2.30pm & 7pm-midnight Ⓜ De Brouckère Ⓥ

Chez Léon (4, E4)

Traditional Belgian €-€€
This Brussels institution is all about the *moules et frites*. It's certainly not about the service (slow) or the ambiance (none). However, the place is open right through from noon until late, so it's a reasonable choice on Rue des Bouchers. Stick to *moules au vin blanc* (mussels with white wine). Kids under 12 eat free when accompanied.

☎ 02 513 04 26 🖳 www.chezleon.be ✉ Rue des Bouchers 18 🕒 noon-11pm Ⓜ De Brouckère 🚇 Bourse ♿

Horta Brasserie Restaurant (3, E3)

Traditional Belgian €€
The restaurant of the Centre Belge de la Bande Dessinée

Lick your plate clean at Belga Queen (p35)

(p14), is worth a lunch stop after perusing the excellent bookshop. Along with the filling brasserie staples, look out for the blackboard specials and the plate of the day – it'll be whatever the locals are having.
☎ 02 217 72 71 ✉ Rue des Sables 20 ☷ 10am-6pm Tue-Sun Ⓜ Gare Centrale

La Maison du Cygne
(4, D5)
French, Modern Belgian €€€€
This elegant restaurant is great for a lunch overlooking the Grand Place (be sure to book a table with a view). There's a brasserie here

Sea Grill

as well (**L'Ommegang**), but smart diners take the business lunch at the restaurant. While the wine menu (with over 20,000 bottles!) and the slightly uptight service might make you squirm, the food will put you at ease.
☎ 02 511 82 44
🖥 www.lamaisonducygne .be ✉ Rue Charles Buls 2 ☷ noon-2pm & 7-10pm Mon-Fri, 7-10pm Sat Ⓜ De Brouckère ⓡ Bourse

Sea Grill (4, F3)
Seafood €€€€
With impeccable credentials (two Michelin stars), Sea Grill is the best seafood restaurant in Brussels (if not all of Belgium). Befitting its starry status, the room is quietly conservative, however the talented chef lets the food do the talking. Great seafood can be complex and still keep that 'fresh from the sea' flavour – something that is achieved with ease here.
☎ 02 227 31 20
🖥 www.seagrill.be
✉ Radisson SAS Hotel, Rue du Fossé aux Loups 47 ☷ noon-2pm & 7-11pm

Mon-Fri, 7pm-midnight Sat Ⓜ De Brouckère

't Kelderke (4, D5)
Traditional Belgian €€
This old cellar restaurant right on the Grand Place serves up hearty portions of traditional fare such as steaming mountains of mussels and *stoemp et saucisses* (mashed potatoes with sausages). While there are no bookings, locals know that this is one worth waiting for.
☎ 02 513 73 44
✉ Grand Place 15 ☷ noon-2am Ⓜ De Brouckère ⓡ Bourse

Waka Moon (4, D6)
African €€
This funky corner café in a converted bookshop serves up African cooking to locals who congregate at the outside tables when the weather permits. There's plenty of chicken on the menu (try the chicken yassa) and the eclectic interior's zebra-striped chairs are happy-snap worthy.
☎ 02 502 10 32
✉ Rue des Eperonniers 60 ☷ 11.30am-3pm & 7-11pm Mon-Fri, 7-11pm Sat Ⓜ Gare Centrale

IXELLES, ST-GILLES & MATONGÉ

Belgo Belge (3, E6)
Bistro-Brasserie €€
One of the new breed of restaurants that have popped up in the Matongé area, this bright, modern eatery serves up mainly Belgian and French classics with a slight twist – try the *waterzooi* or the *magret de canard* (duck).
☎ 02 511 11 21 ☐ www .belgobelge.be ✉ Rue de la Pay 20 ⏰ noon-2.30pm & 7-11.30pm Mon-Fri, 7-11.30pm Sat & Sun M Porte de Namur

Eat & Love (3, E6)
Vietnamese/Thai €-€€
We've long since stopped questioning why Brussels has such a plethora of restaurants with both Vietnamese and Thai sharing the same menu, but we've given this stylish little place the benefit of the doubt because it does both so well. Try the excellent Vietnamese *pho* (soup) with beef and the delectable Thai red curry chicken.
☎ 02 513 64 73 ✉ Rue St-Boniface 11 ⏰ noon-2.30pm & 7-11pm, closed Sun & lunch Sat M Porte de Namur V

En Face de Parachute (6, B3)
Bistro €€
A warm and inviting space, with bottle-lined walls and a serving counter where the chefs deliver their fantastic plates, awaits the locals who keep flocking back to this great eatery. The freshest

MOULES ET FRITES
The country's national dish is *moules et frites* – mussels and fries. The mussels, mostly from the Netherlands, are cooked in either a stock or white wine and arrive with a generous serving of fries (see p83) – adding to the challenge in getting through the dish. Some common mussel dishes (served steaming in a pot) are *moules marinières* (with wine, garlic, onion and herbs), *vin blanc* (with white wine), *à la provençale* (with tomato) and *à la bière* (cooked in beer and cream). Follow the local rule of thumb and eat shellfish only during months with an 'r' in the name and discard any that haven't opened properly once cooked.

ingredients and wonderful, detailed preparation are the keys – try the tartare of Japanese tuna and a hearty meat dish for a main. Bookings are essential. No credit cards.
☎ 02 346 47 41 ✉ Chaussée de Waterloo 578 ⏰ noon-2pm & 7-10pm Tue-Sat ☐ Horta V

La Quincaillerie (6, A2)
Seafood, Modern Belgian €€€
One of the most unique and handsome eateries in Brussels, this former metal-wares shop (quincaillerie means hardware) is a feast for the

eyes, with its metal gang-ways and central antique clock keeping time. By 9pm every night the waiters are run off their feet delivering seafood delights to hungry locals and businesspeople.
☎ 02 533 98 33 ☐ www.quincaillerie .be ✉ Rue du Page 45 ⏰ noon-2.30pm & 7pm-midnight Mon-Fri, 7pm-midnight Sat & Sun M Porte de Hal ☐ Horta V

Le Fils de Jules (6, A2)
Basque €€
This is the kind of local favourite where the staff

Former hardware shop La Quincaillerie scrubbed up nicely

JEAN-BERNARD CARILLET

WAYNE WALTON

DICEY DINING

While Rue des Bouchers (just off the Grand Place) may look enticing at night, the strike rate of good eateries here is pretty slim. All of these fixed-price menus, pretty pictures and seafood on ice disguise the fact that most eateries here are underwhelming. If you're not a culinary gambler, try **Aux Armes de Bruxelles** (p35) for smart seafood or **Chez Léon** (p35) for typical mussel dishes.

and the affluent clientele know each other so well that a menu isn't necessary. The Deco-esque setting is understated, allowing the excellent food to shine. While the menu is seasonal, expect plenty of *foie gras* dishes (divine with lentils), beautiful fresh fish and some great wines (some Basque).
☎ 02 534 00 57
🖳 www.filsdejules.be in French ✉ cnr Rue du Page & Rue Américaine 🕑 noon-2.30pm & 7-11pm, 7-11pm Sat & Sun 🚇 Horta

Mano & Mano (3, E6)
Italian €€
On Rue St-Boniface, Brussels newest 'eat street', this simple Italian restaurant headed up by two Sicilian chefs does great business serving up good-value fresh pastas, salads and tasty pizzas late into the night.
☎ 02 502 08 01
✉ Rue St-Boniface 8

🕑 noon-2.30pm & 6.30pm-midnight, 6.30pm-midnight Sat-Sun 🚇 Porte de Namur

Rouge Tomate (6, B1)
International €€€
Rouge Tomate has a rosy glow feel that's as fresh as the food on offer. Start off with a light dish such as the marinated scallops and move on to one of the excellent fish or pasta mains. There are small vineyard wines on offer and outdoor seating when the weather cooperates.
☎ 02 647 70 44
🖳 www.rougetomate.be
✉ Ave Louise 190
🕑 noon-2.30pm & 7-10.30pm, closed Sun & lunch Sat 🚇 Louise 🅥

Tchin Tchin (6, A2)
Thai €€
This modish little Thai-Viet restaurant pleases local Thai aficionados with its authentic

(and well-priced) dishes such as chu chi prawns and duck curry.
☎ 02 534 00 73 ✉ Rue Américaine 89 🕑 noon-2.30pm & 7-11pm, closed Sun & lunch Sat
🚇 Horta 🅥

Toucan Brasserie (6, A3)
French/Belgian €€
The contemporary brasserie fare on offer at this traditional-looking restaurant has plenty of local fans – so book ahead. Try the tasty shrimp croquettes first and something meaty to follow up, while vegetarians can try the short but surefooted vegetarian menu. This is a fantastic place in the warmer months when tables fill the footpath.
☎ 02 345 30 17
🖳 www.toucanbrasserie.com ✉ Ave Louis Lepoutre 1 🕑 noon-2.30pm & 7-11pm, closed Sun & lunch Sat
🚇 Horta 🅥

MAROLLES

Brasserie Ploegmans
(3, C5)
Traditional Belgian €€
This authentic working-class bar is a classic, filled with crusty regulars who bemoan the fact that the food's gone all trendy. However, while the white plates and presentation add an air of sophistication, thankfully the food here remains rustic. Try the *stoemp et saucisses* or the entrecôte.
☎ 02 503 21 24 ⊠ Rue Haute 148 ⌚ 11am-10pm Ⓜ Louise

Comme Chez Soi (3, C4)
French, Modern Belgian €€€€
This family-run business has had three Michelin stars for years and the often inventive cuisine has kept with the times, while the Art Nouveau décor remains just as it should. It's hard to get evening bookings, so on short notice your best bet is a lunch reservation. Foodies should book a kitchen table.
☎ 02 512 29 21
🖳 www.commechezsoi.be ⊠ Place Rouppe 23 ⌚ noon-1.30pm & 7-9.30pm Tue-Sat Ⓜ Gare du Midi 🚌 Anneessens Ⓥ

La Grande Porte (3, C5)
Traditional Belgian €€
This fun old bistro gets livelier as the night wears on and the bowls of traditional onion soup leave the kitchen more frequently. The cuisine is happily ensconced in the past and once you try such favourites as the *ballekes aux Mariolennes* (Marolles meatballs) you'll want it to stay that way.
☎ 02 512 89 98 ⊠ Rue Notre-Seigneur 9 ⌚ noon-

Try your best to get into Comme Chez Soi

3pm & 6pm-2am Mon-Fri, 6pm-2am Sat Ⓜ Porte de Hal

SABLON

Le Bilboquet (3, D5)
Café/Restaurant €-€€
This casual eatery just off Place du Grand Sablon is where hip locals come with their newspapers (yes, they still read them) and have a coffee or two before their friends turn up, and dig into the great salads, pizzas and pasta dishes. Buzzy and fun.
☎ 02 513 74 40 ⊠ Rue Lebeau 69 ⌚ kitchen noon-2.30pm & 7-10.30pm, to 4pm Sun; drinks 9am-11pm Ⓜ Porte de Namur Ⓥ

Le Perroquet (3, D5)
Café €-€€
It's actually a shame that this place is always so crowded with locals chowing down on spicy pittas or salads washed down with beer – not just

because it's sometimes hard to get a table, but because you'd like to check out the charming Art Nouveau décor more closely.
☎ 02 512 99 22 ⊠ Rue Watteeu 31 ⌚ 10.30am-midnight Ⓜ Louise Ⓥ

Lola (3, D5)
Brasserie €€€
Filled to breaking point with an arty clientele for weekend lunches, Lola has become an institution and despite being around a few years it still feels contemporary. The excellent menu offers dishes as light or heavy as you want to go and the wine list (including some New World wines) is well chosen.
☎ 02 514 24 60
🖳 www.restolola.be in French ⊠ Place du Grand Sablon 33 ⌚ noon-3pm & 6.30-11.30pm Mon-Fri, noon-11.30pm Sat & Sun Ⓜ Porte de Namur Ⓥ

Ballekes aux Mariolennes at La Grande Porte

Industrial chic at La Manufacture

STE-CATHERINE

De Noordzee/La Mer du Nord (4, B3)
Seafood €-€€
This fresh seafood shop has a wonderful stall at the front of it that tempts passers-by with its aromatic soups and attracts locals who frequent it to down some fresh oysters (standing up) accompanied by a crisp white wine. Fresh, fast and fun.
☎ 02 513 11 92
✉ Rue Ste-Catherine 45
◷ 8am-6pm Tue-Fri, 8am-5pm Sat Ⓜ Ste-Catherine

Le Fourneau (4, B2)
French/Belgian €€
With a layout that echoes Paris' L'Atelier de Joël Robuchon, where diners perch on bar stools around an open kitchen, Le Fourneau does brisk business serving up tasting-sized servings of seafood and meat (ordered in multiples of 100g). After sampling the cute portions (€5) of fresh seafood, you can move on to main courses or just keep grazing the menu.
☎ 02 513 10 02 ✉ Place Ste-Catherine 8 ◷ noon-

2.30 & 6.30 onwards, closed Sun lunch & Tue
Ⓜ Ste-Catherine

La Manufacture (3, B3)
French, International €€-€€€
Formerly a Delvaux (famous for their handbags) workshop, La Manufacture's stylish industrial setting is host to suits for power lunches and a more fashionable crowd at night. The food is French with the occasional Med or Asian twist – but not that diners here really notice – the setting and people-watching takes pride of place.
☎ 02 502 25 25
🖳 www.manufacture.be in French ✉ Rue Notre-Dame du Sommeil 12 ◷ noon-2pm & 7-11pm Mon-Fri, 7pm-midnight Sat
Ⓜ Ste-Catherine Ⓥ

Le Vistro (4, B2)
Seafood €€€
This petite seafood eatery is best experienced when the weather allows for alfresco dining to be set up on the square opposite. While there are plenty of *homard* (lobster) and fish dishes on the menu, we find it hard to ever go past the *moules marinières*

with their delicious fries on the side.
☎ 02 512 41 81
🖳 www.levistro.be in French ✉ Quai aux Briques 16 ◷ 12.30-2.30pm & from 6.30pm Ⓜ Ste-Catherine

Little Asia (4, B3)
Vietnamese €€
This funky eatery has been such a hit that they're open from lunch to 11pm on Saturdays to stop a (polite) Belgian riot. The reason, besides the hip décor, is the long authentic (enough) menu and fantastic flavours of Vietnam on offer. Try the assorted entrées or the beef *pho* for starters and take it from there.
☎ 02 502 88 36
🖳 www.littleasia.be
✉ Rue Ste-Catherine 8
◷ noon-3pm & 6-11pm Mon-Fri, noon-11pm Sat
Ⓜ Ste-Catherine Ⓥ

Vismet (4, C2)
Seafood €€-€€€
Ushering in a newer breed of seafood restaurant in Ste-Catherine, this understated, open-kitchen seafood restaurant has gained a good reputation for its fresh fish dishes. The fish soup makes a

great starter if it's cold out and ordering any of the fish main courses is the best approach.
☎ 02 218 85 45 ☒ Place Ste-Catherine 23 ☽ noon-2.30 & 7-11pm Tue-Sat Ⓜ Ste-Catherine

ST-GÉRY

Bonsoir Clara (4, B3)
French, International €€€
The perfect stop on boutique-lined Rue Antoine Dansaert, the two attractive dining rooms here accommodate a fashionable clientele who delight in the seasonal menu (there are some great set menus too) that always features great fish dishes and a focused wine list.
☎ 02 502 09 90 ⌨ www .bonsoirclara.be in French ☒ Rue Antoine Dansaert 22 ☽ noon-2.30pm & 7-11.30pm Mon-Thu, 2.30pm & 7pm-midnight Fri, 7-11.30pm Sat & Sun Ⓜ Ste-Catherine ⓥ Bourse Ⓥ

In 't Spinnekopke (3, B3)
Traditional Belgian €€-€€€
This old coach inn, dating from the 18th century, is

Kasbah

Dine like royalty at Belga Queen

worth seeking out for those after a 'true' Brussels eatery of old. Arrive with a healthy appetite to try one of the classic beer-soaked Belgian mains such as *pintadeau à la bière de framboise* (guinea-fowl in raspberry beer).
☎ 02 511 86 95 ⌨ www .spinnekopke.be ☒ Place du Jardin aux Fleurs 1 ☽ 11am-11pm Mon-Fri, 6pm-midnight Sat Ⓜ Ste-Catherine ⓥ Bourse

Kasbah (4, B3)
Middle Eastern €€
The favourite Middle East eatery of the fashion district (where, of course, *everyone's* been to Morocco on a photo shoot) in downtown Brussels, the Kasbah does a decent approximation of Middle East favourites such as tasty mezze and steaming couscous while sipping Moroccan wine.
☎ 02 502 40 26 ☒ Rue Antoine Dansaert 20 ☽ noon-3pm & 6.30pm-midnight Ⓜ Ste-Catherine ⓥ Bourse Ⓥ

Le Bar à Tapas (4, B5)
Spanish €-€€
The good-value tapas on offer at this friendly tapas bar attracts a local crowd who've usually been sipping beers just down the corner at Roi des Belges (p45). No real surprises on the menu and if you're really peckish (or imbibed a little too much) they do a decent paella.
☎ 02 502 66 02 ⌨ www .baratapas.be ☒ Borgval 11 ☽ noon-12.30am Mon-Fri, 6pm-late Sat & Sun Ⓜ De Brouckère ⓥ Bourse Ⓥ

Le Pain Quotidien (4, B3)
Bakery €
This *boulangerie* (bakery) is perfect for a quick snack or for sipping a coffee while reading a magazine at its long communal table. Excellent sandwiches.
☎ 02 502 23 61 ⌨ www.painquotidien.com ☒ Rue Antoine Dansaert 16 ☽ 7.30am-6pm Ⓜ Ste-Catherine ⓥ Bourse ♿ ✕

Like a good old-fashioned all-round entertainer, Brussels sure can perform – with one toe-tapping heel in the past and another in the future, she can sing, dance, strum a guitar, tell a joke, often all at once!

On any one night you can swig Belgian beer at a century-old pub, sip coffee in a faded brown café, down cocktails at a contemporary bar, see theatre in an Art Deco palace, or listen to classical music at a circus!

Brussels doesn't distinguish between cafés, bars and pubs as many global cities do and sometimes they're all rolled into one. Brown cafés are actually small old-fashioned pubs, while *estaminets* are traditional cafés and can get as rowdy as a typical London pub some nights. At either you could comfortably have a cup of coffee while your friend sips *jenever* (Belgian gin). Performing arts venues are no different – at Halles de Schaerbeek (p48) or the Beursschouwburg (p47) you're just as likely to see contemporary theatre and dance, as you are live music and a DJ set.

Entertainment opportunities are everywhere although the area around the Grand Place and Place St-Géry is home to most cafés, bars, and jazz clubs while Rue du Marché au Charbon is the centre of the gay scene.

Not all the fun is indoors, especially during summer when Brussels moves outdoors. Cafés set up sun terraces, dance parties are held in parks and there are myriad open-air events, especially in the Grand Place, host to concerts and spectacles such as the Tapis des Fleurs (Carpet of Flowers), when the cobblestones can't be seen for begonias.

Brussels is not a seven-days-a-week city. Although there's always something on somewhere, most live music events and clubbing action happens at weekends with some dance clubs only opening Friday and Saturday nights. For most Bruxellois it's all work during the week with play saved for weekends, when they really let their hair down – going out at midnight and staying out till dawn is the norm for the clubbing set, while the older crowd enjoy long afternoons on a sunny café terrace and an evening at a concert or theatre.

Enjoy some Sunday afternoon jazz at La Brocante (p44)

EVENTS CALENDAR

March
Ars Musica (www.arsmusica.be) – contemporary music festival

May
Brussels Jazz Marathon (www.brussels jazzmarathon.be) – highly respected jazz festival held all over the city

Kunsten Festival des Arts (www .kunstenfestivaldesarts.be) – Flemish and Wallonian festival of arts & culture

Belgian Lesbian & Gay Pride (www .blgp.be) – also called Pink Saturday, a full-on glamour parade

June
Ommegang (www.ommegang.be) – three days of medieval festivities with a grand procession from Place du Grand Sablon to Grand Place

Couleur Café Festival (www.couleur café.be) – three-day festival of world music and dance

July
Festival du Film Bruxelles (www.fffb .be) –10-day festival of European cinema

Foire de Midi – Europe's largest travelling fun fair spends the summer on Blvd du Midi

Belgium National Day – independence day celebrations centred on Parc de Bruxelles

Festival de Midis-Minimes (www .midis-minimes.be) – festival of chamber, baroque and choral music

August
Brussels Marathon (www.sport.be) – join thousands to pound the capital's cobblestones

Tapis des Fleurs – a brilliant floral carpet of 800,000 begonias is laid out across the Grand Place

September
Belgian Beer Weekend – beer-tasting extravaganza centred around the Grand Place

December
Marché de Noël – gorgeous Christmas markets are held in the Grand Place every winter

CAFÉS, BARS & PUBS

À la Mort Subite (4, F4)
While 'instant death' may be the name of this wonderful Art Nouveau bar (and also the name of a beer), the place still has a lot of life in it. Four generations of the Vossen family have ran this convivial café close to Galerie Royales St-Hubert, making it ideally placed for a break mid-shopping.
☎ 02 513 13 18 ⌨ www .alamortsubite.be ⌂ Rue Montagne aux Herbes Potagères 7, Lower Town ⏱ 11am-midnight Ⓜ Gare Centrale

Au Cercle des Voyageurs (4, C6)
This colonial-style café with comfy armchairs, potted palm trees, delicious cakes, an excellent travel library and Internet access also hosts travel photography exhibitions, lectures and presentations on journeys, and language and tango lessons.
☎ 02 514 39 49 ⌨ www .lecercledesvoyageurs.com ⌂ Rue des Grands Carmes 18 ⏱ 11am-late ⌂ Anneessens

Café Central (4, B4)
While the décor of this dark bar is traditional – very cosy

on a winter's night – its avant garde attitude makes it anything but! Expect eclectic events each night – art house films on Sunday, quirky DJs Thursday to Saturday and live experimental musical on Monday and Wednesday.
☎ 0486 72 26 24 ⌂ Rue Borgval 14, St-Géry ⏱ 11am-late Ⓜ Ste-Catherine ⌂ Bourse

Café Métropole (4, E2)
Hôtel Métropole's café-bar is the grand old lady of Brussels' café scene, with its wonderful high ornate ceilings, enormous glass chandeliers, padded red

SOLO TRAVELLERS

Sublime places for…

- people-watching on a sunny afternoon – Roi des Belges (opposite)
- enjoying coffee over a comic book on your own – Walvis (p46)
- meeting friendly Leffe-swigging locals – Café Central (p43)
- sharing tales of the ridiculous with fellow travellers – Au Cercle des Voyageurs (p43)

JEAN-BERNARD CARILLET

leather seats, elegant red lampshades and giant picture windows – just perfect for aperitifs and people-watching.

☎ 02 219 23 84 ⊠ Place de Brouckère 31 ☼ 9am-1am Sun-Thu, 9am-2am Fri & Sat Ⓜ De Brouckère

Cirio (4, C4)

The thing to drink at this splendid Belle Époque café, with its striped banquette seating, wall mirrors and brass coat-stands, is a *half-en-half,* an elegant combination champagne and white wine.

☎ 02 512 13 95 ⊠ Rue de la Bourse 20, Bourse ☼ 10am-midnight Ⓜ Ste-Catherine Ⓡ Bourse

Daringman (4, A2)

A laid-back neighbourhood pub where privileged young arts students mix with an older, working-class crowd – Daringman is the place to head to when you want to kick back with a Belgian brew and chat to some affable locals.

☎ 02 512 43 23 ⊠ Rue de Flandre 37, Ste-Catherine ☼ noon-1am Tue-Thu, noon-2am Fri, 4pm-2am Sat Ⓜ Ste-Catherine

Falstaff (4, C4)

The fine woodwork enhancing the ornate stained glass at this elegant Art Nouveau café is no doubt exceptionally graceful as it was carved by Horta's carpenter when he helped the original owner decorate her brasserie in 1903. It's naturally appropriate to order a *half-en-half* here too.

☎ 02 511 87 89 🖳 www .resto.be/minisites/falstaff ⊠ Rue Henri Maus 19, Lower Town ☼ 10am-2am Ⓜ De Brouckère Ⓡ Bourse

Fin de Siècle (4, A4)

Another wonderful traditional bar of the kind Brussels does so well – this one made hip by the changing displays of art on the walls and cool

TERRY CARTER

MERCI DU DMHA (?)

La Brocante

sounds. The laidback vibe, friendly staff and hearty pub grub make this popular with locals who line up for tables.

☎ 02 513 51 23 ⊠ Rue des Chartreux 9, St-Géry ☼ 5pm-3pm Ⓜ Ste-Catherine Ⓡ Bourse

Goupil le Fol (4, D6)

Visitors to this whimsically decorated bar, with its faded charm and old bric-a-brac, find the nostalgic atmosphere either immensely appealing or incredibly irritating – despite requests to put on other kinds of music, the owner only plays French *chansons,* the cabaret music popularised by Piaf and Brel.

☎ 02 511 13 96 ⊠ Rue de la Violette 22, Lower Town ☼ 8pm-5am Ⓜ Gare Centrale

La Brocante (3, C6)

This smoky neighbourhood bar, with enormous picture windows overlooking the daily flea market, gets crowded with genial locals, especially on Sunday afternoons, when they cram in to listen to a talented Gypsy family play excellent Django Reinhardt–style jazz guitar.

☎ 02 512 13 43 ⊠ Rue Blaes, Marolles ☼ 5am-7pm Ⓜ Louise

L'Archiduc (4, B4)

Step inside this swish Art Deco lounge and you'll feel like you've stepped onto a 1940s Hollywood film set. Started in 1937 by Brussels jazz pioneer Stan Brenders (who worked with Django Reinhardt), Charlie Parker and Nat King Cole performed here in its early days and for many the 5pm 'after-shopping' weekend jazz gigs are Brussels at its best.
☎ 02 512 06 52 ✉ Rue Antoine Dansaert 6, Lower Town 🕑 4pm-5am Ⓜ Ste-Catherine 🚊 Bourse

Le Greenwich (4, B4)

If you can divert your attention from the intense games of chess – players meet daily to compete at this smoke-filled, high-ceilinged café (chess legends Bobby Fischer and Garry Kasparov are said to have played here) – grab a window seat for great people-watching in this fashion quarter.
☎ 02 511 41 67 ✉ Rue des Chartreux 7, Lower Town 🕑 10am-1am Sun-Thu, 10am-2am Fri & Sat Ⓜ Ste-Catherine 🚊 Bourse

L'Ultime Atome (3, E6)

This large buzzy neighbourhood café on a street full of great cafés and bistros is popular with locals and expats, especially families, who can let their kids go crazy – nobody cares, it's all so convivial.
☎ 02 511 16 59 ✉ Rue des Alexiens 53, Lower Town 🕑 11am-8pm Ⓜ Gare Centrale 🚊 Anneessens

Mezzo (4, B4)

While the faded colonial gentlemen's club feel of this two-floor bar – with lots of dark wood, Chesterfield sofas, warm glowing lamps and framed pictures on the walls – seems at odds with the DJ's rarefied global sounds, it somehow works very nicely.
☎ 02 646 53 94 ✉ Rue Borgval 18, Lower Town 🕑 11am-late Ⓜ Ste-Catherine 🚊 Bourse

Roi des Belges (4, B4)

The next-best summer terrace after Zebra (p46; which has the bonus of live music), with friendly staff and cheap snacks, but if you can't get

L'Archiduc

a seat here, head across to **Mappa Mundo** (4, B4; ☎ 02 514 35 55). All three are owned by entrepreneur Frédéric Nicolay, who's responsible for transforming Place St-Géry into the scene it is today.
☎ 02 503 43 00 ✉ Rue Jules Van Praet 35, Lower Town 🕑 11am-late Ⓜ De Brouckère 🚊 Bourse

Rosa (3, D5)

Recently changing its emphasis away from food to focus on lounging, drinking and dancing, Rosa's funky vibrant design has fortunately kept the same feel – lots of big round colourful ottomans, Kartel's lolly-pop Perspex chairs and colourful shagpile cushions to lounge on.
☎ 02 513 08 07 ✉ Blvd de Waterloo 36-7 🕑 7pm-late Ⓜ Louise

Roy d'Espagne (4, D5)

This atmospheric pub is without a doubt the best drinking option on the gorgeous Grand Place – with wonderful fireplaces keeping the place warm in winter. It's nevertheless needlessly expensive and probably only

Mappa Mundo's massive menu

Get into the groove at Fuse

warrants a drink or two to enjoy the phenomenal views.
☎ 02 513 08 07 ✉ Grand Place 1, Lower Town ⏰ 10am-1am Ⓜ Bourse

Walvis (3, B2)
With its buzzy vibe, cheap drinks, free weekly concerts – everything from cabaret to Iranian percussion – and DJs spinning soul, jazz and retro three nights a week, Walvis is popular with local students and artists in this interesting immigrant neighbourhood (check out the Bollywood tape shops down the street).
☎ 02 512 43 23 ✉ Rue Antoine Dansaert 209 ⏰ 11am-2am Ⓜ Ste-Catherine

Zebra (4, D4)
While there are few things more sublime than sitting in the sunshine of a summer terrace at Place St-Géry, sipping a glass of white wine and listening to live jazz, the watchful crowds waiting for the place's most-coveted spot sometimes make it hard to relax.
☎ 02 511 09 01 ✉ Place St-Géry 33-35, Lower Town ⏰ 11am-1am Ⓜ De Brouckère ⓑ Bourse

DANCE CLUBS

Bazaar (3, C5)
The exotic upstairs restaurant (with a brocade hot-air balloon over the bar) is transformed into a buzzy lounge bar after midnight, while the colourful cavernous basement club gets crammed with locals and expats dancing to disco, soul and funk.
☎ 02 511 26 00 ✉ Rue des Capucins 63, Marolles € €8 ⏰ midnight-late Thu-Sat Ⓜ Porte de Hal

Fuse (3, C6)
This state of the art club spread over several floors, with cool ice box lighting and disco balls, is Brussels' biggest and one of Europe's best for techno and house, and crams clubbers in on weekends.
☎ 02 511 97 89 ✉ www .fuse.be ✉ Rue Blaes 208, Marolles € 11pm-midnight €2.50, midnight-7am €8 ⏰ 11pm-7am Sat Ⓜ Porte de Hal

Mirano (3, F3)
Dirty Dancing at Mirano is the kind of club all clubs should be like: glam design, gorgeous people, great vibe and good music – mainly

techno and deep house. Dress your best for the style police or you won't get in.
☎ 02 227 39 48 ✉ www .mirano.be, www.dirty dancing.be ✉ Chaussée de Louvain 38, St-Josse € 10-11pm free, 11pm-midnight €5, midnight-4am €10, doors close 4-6am ⏰ 10pm-6am Sat, occasionally on Fri Ⓜ Madou

CINEMAS

Cinéma Arenberg-Galeries (4, E5)
This art house theatre offers up an eclectic programme of world cinema, excellent retrospectives and classics.
☎ 02 512 80 63 ✉ www .arenberg.be in French & Dutch ✉ Galerie de la Reine 26, Lower Town € €6.60/5.20 Ⓜ Gare Centrale ♿ fair ⓧ

UGC Cinéma (4, D1)
If you're hanging out for some commercial cinema, the 12 theatres here should satisfy your craving.
☎ 0900 104 40 ✉ www .ugc.be in French & Dutch ✉ Place de Brouckère 38, Lower Town € €7.20/5.60 Ⓜ De Brouckère

Get your jazz fix at Music Village

ROCK, JAZZ & BLUES

Ancienne Belgique
(4, B5)
Unquestionably Brussels' coolest concert venue, for the sound quality and the sound quality acts (everyone from Goldfrapp to Death Cab for Cutie) but also for the management: it never gets too crowded, the great balconies allow everyone good sightlines, an upstairs club hosts local bands and people hang around the bar afterwards discussing the show – love it!
☎ 02 548 24 24 🖳 www .abconcerts.be ✉ Blvd

Anspach 110, Lower Town; box office: Rue des Pierres 23 € varies depending on act ⊙ box office 11am-6pm & after 7pm Ⓜ De Brouckère 🚋 Bourse

Music Village (4, C5)
Enjoy a wide variety of jazz here (from jazz legends doing be-bop and blues to young experimentalists fusing jazz with other rhythms) along with flamenco, fado and French *chansons*. Amateur jazz singers take to the stage on Tuesday.
☎ 02 513 13 45 🖳 www .themusicvillage.com ✉ Rue des Pierres 50, Lower Town € €7.50-24 ⊙ dinner

7pm & concerts 9pm Tue-Sat Ⓜ De Brouckère 🚋 Bourse

Sounds Jazz Club (3, F6)
Get on down to this low-key, smoke-filled jazz club – Brussels oldest – in the African neighbourhood of Ixelles, to groove to the most adventurous jazz around, almost every night of the week.
☎ 02 512 92 50 ✉ Rue de la Tulipe 28, Ixelles € free-€15 ⊙ 7pm-1am Mon-Fri, 10pm-1am Sat Ⓜ Porte de Namur

MUSIC, OPERA & PERFORMING ARTS

Beursschouwburg (4, B4)
The Beursschouwburg is back with a bang after a brilliant refurbishment to continue to host challenging con-temporary and world-music concerts, theatre, dance, photography, animation, art and mixed media events, along with forums on design, architecture, literature, politics and films, in English, Dutch or French. The funky

LET BELGIANS ENTERTAIN YOU...
- Adolphe Sax (1814–94) invented the saxophone in 1842 – hear some at the Music Village (above).
- Jacques Brel (1929–78) began in Brussels cabaret... see cabaret of a campier kind at Chez Maman (p48).
- Django Reinhardt (1910–53) was a jazz guitar great... tap your toes to gypsy jazz Sundays at La Brocante (p44).
- Audrey Hepburn (1929–93), Hollywood screen legend, was born in Brussels... enjoy classic films at the Musée du Cinéma (p20).
- Johnny Hallyday (1943–, of Belgian parentage) is considered by the French to be their king of rock 'n' roll... catch some at Ancienne Belgique (above).
- Jean-Claude Van Damme (1960–) kicked butt in Hollywood action flicks... if you must, try the UGC Cinéma (opposite).

Bubbling Théâtre Royal de la Monnaie

Beurs Café has DJs from 7pm, Wednesday to Saturday.
☎ 02 550 03 50 🖳 www
.beursschouwburg.be in
French & Dutch ✉ Rue
Auguste Orts 20-28, Lower
Town € from €8.50 ⏲ box
office 10am-6pm Mon-Fri
Ⓜ De Brouckère Ⓑ Bourse

BOZAR/Palais des Beaux-Arts (3, E4)
Victor Horta's gorgeous
Art Deco palace, reborn as
BOZAR, is now a vibrant
Centre for Fine Arts, with
an exciting programme
of classical music (from
chamber music to symphony
orchestras), Belgian jazz, innovative dance and theatre
(occasionally in English),
along with challenging
art exhibitions and film,
architecture and literary
events.
☎ info 02 507 84 44, tickets
02 507 82 00 🖳 www.bozar
.be ✉ Rue Ravenstein 23,
Upper Town € varies
⏲ box office 11am-7pm
Mon-Sat, to 5pm summer
Ⓜ Parc

Cirque Royal (3, E3)
This luxe performance space
sees everything in its venue
from classical and contemporary music, to world music

and comedy (sometimes in
English).
☎ 02 218 20 15 ✉ Rue de
l'Enseignement 81, Upper
Town € €10-85 ⏲ box
office 10.30am-6pm Mon-Sat
& 1hr before performances
Ⓜ Madou

Halles de Schaerbeek (3, F1)
The wonderful site of the
former Marché Ste-Marie
food market, dating back to
1901, is now a performing
arts venue for provocative
contemporary music, dance,
circus, mixed media events,
films and installations.
☎ 02 218 21 07 🖳 www
.halles.be in French ✉ Rue
Royale Ste-Marie 22a,
Schaerbeek; box office:
Rue de la Constitution 20
€ €10-35 ⏲ box office
2-6pm Mon-Fri Ⓜ Botanique

Le Botanique (3, F2)
Make an effort to catch a
performance or concert
here – classical orchestras
and choirs to indie pop/rock
and world music – the setting is magical. The Centre
Culturel de la Communauté
Francaise (French Com-
munity Cultural Centre) has
converted a greenhouse
into a number of wonderful

spaces with lush fernery
intact. The cellar-like Witlof
Bar is a must!
☎ 02 218 37 32, 02 226 12
11 🖳 www.botanique.be in
French & Dutch ✉ Rue Roy-
ale 236, St-Josse € €10-40
⏲ box office 10.30am-6pm
Mon-Sat Ⓜ Botanique

Théâtre Royal de la Monnaie (4, E3)
The elegant neoclassical
façade is unfortunately all
that remains of the original
La Monnaie, Belgium's
premier opera house, built
in 1817 but razed by fire
in 1855. Fortunately that
doesn't prevent you from
seeing exceptional opera.
☎ 02 229 12 00, box office
070 23 39 39 🖳 www
.lamonnaie.be ✉ Place de
la Monnaie, Lower Town
€ performances €7.50-150;
opera house tours €6/3/4
⏲ box office 11am-6pm
Tue-Sat; tours noon Sat
Sep-Dec & Mar-Jun Ⓜ De
Brouckère

GAY & LESBIAN BRUSSELS

Chez Maman (4, B6)
This legendary cabaret bar
welcomes gay and straight
alike to their exuberant drag
shows by the most fabulous
queens in the business!
☎ 02 502 86 96 ✉ Rue
des Grands Carmes 7, Lower
Town € from €8 ⏲ 10pm-
late Thu-Sun Ⓜ De
Brouckère Ⓑ Bourse

Fontainas (4, B6)
Many people's favourite
Charbon spot (for gay and
straight alike), the friendly
staff, smooth music and retro
décor give the bar its relaxed

GETTING OUT

Tickets to concerts, cultural and sporting events can be bought from FNAC (in City 2, p27; ☎ 0900 00600) if not from the box office at the venue itself. To find out what's on, check out *The Bulletin* magazine's *What's On* supplement (in English), and pick up free guides, like *ZONE02, Agenda,* or *Rif Raf* (www.rifraf.be) from cafés, bars and pubs. All have entertainment listings and reviews. Most are in French or Dutch, but you'll still be able to identify what's on when – if not, just ask a friendly local.

vibe. Sunday Tea Time from 3pm is fun.
☎ 02 503 31 12 ✉ Rue du Marché au Charbon 91, Lower Town € from €8 ⊙ 11am-2am late Thu-Sun 🚇 Anneessens or Bourse

La Démence (3, C6)

Fuse (p46) lets 'the Madness' take over once or twice a month with boys bussing in from all over Europe for decadent partying, over three levels including two dance floors, several dark rooms, a few bars, go-go dancers, massages and lots of foam.
☎ 02 511 97 89 🖳 www .lademence.com ✉ Fuse, Rue Blaes 208, Marolles € 10-11pm €8, 11pm-noon €13 ⊙ 10pm-noon once or twice a month 🚇 Porte de Hal

Le Belgica (4, C5)

Get down to this friendly, atmospheric bar, a gay institution in Brussels, for DJs spinning house and funk, with Sunday's legendary 'Landing' night of jazz, soul and soft electronica being especially fun.
🖳 www.lebelgica.be ✉ Rue du Marché au Charbon 32, Lower Town ⊙ 10pm-3am Thu-Sat, 7pm-3am Sun 🚇 De Brouckère 🚇 Bourse

L'Homo Erectus (4, C5)

There's something fabulous going down almost every night of the week at this popular bar, from flamboyant drag shows to steamy dance nights.
☎ 02 514 74 93 🖳 www .lhomoerectus.com ✉ Rue des Pierres 57, Lower Town

⊙ noon-6am Mon-Fri, 2pm-6am Sat & Sun 🚇 De Brouckère 🚇 Bourse

Maison Arc-en-Ciel

(4, C5)
Maison Arc-en-Ciel (Rainbow House) is a friendly gay and lesbian meeting point and bar (on a street that is thumping with gay bars) where you can get the latest info on one-off parties and regular happenings, such as those held by lesbian collective Mega Top Biches (www.mega-top-biches.org) and Sunday tea dances (big in Brussels).
☎ 02 503 11 60 🖳 www .rainbowhouse.be ✉ Rue du Marché au Charbon, Lower Town ⊙ 6.30-10.30pm Wed-Sat 🚇 De Brouckère 🚇 Bourse

SPORTS

Roi Baudouin Stadium

Brussels' 50,000-seat stadium is the venue for international football matches, major sporting events, and big gigs, such as U2 and the Rolling Stones.
☎ 02 474 39 40 🖳 www .prosportevent.be ✉ Ave du Marathon, Heysel € €10-85 🚇 Roi Baudouin

Vanden Stock Stadium

If you're a keen football fan, try to go see the city's most famous team, the purple-jerseyed RSC Anderlecht, play at their home ground.
☎ 02 529 40 67 🖳 www .anderlecht-online.be ✉ Ave Théo Verbeeck 2, Anderlecht € football tickets €7-28 ⊙ box office 10am-5.30pm Mon-Fri, 10am-noon Sat 🚇 St-Guidon

Have a ball at Vanden Stock stadium

Hotels in Brussels tend to be on the expensive side due to the number of Eurocrats and journalists whose expense accounts make it a win-win situation for them and the hotels during the week. In Europe's summer months, from May to September, however, Brussels is filled to the gills with travellers taking advantage of the discounted rooms. For the weekend traveller visiting Brussels, this translates to excellent bargains in some pretty flash hotels (see box, p54).

From budget to deluxe accommodation, you'll find Brussels' hotels, hostels and B&Bs clean and friendly. Levels of facilities might vary in the midrange hotels (although many are starting to feature free wi-fi), however, it's easy to overlook this when hotels such as Hotel Mozart (p53) have such distinct personalities. Some of the top-end and deluxe hotels are independently run and exceptional by any standards – particularly the Hotel Amigo (opposite).

Art Nouveau reigns supreme in Brussels

You'll find breakfasts in all but the best hotels to be a typically underwhelming cold buffet – not the best way to start the day after some heavy Belgian beers – and only some have dedicated restaurants, although that's not a great problem in Brussels. Facilities for the disabled are finally starting to improve in Brussels and we've noted those offering decent facilities. Finally, Brussels is starting to realise that paying for a room that reeks like your clubbing clothes after stumbling in at 7am is not a desirable thing and now several hotels have dedicated nonsmoking floors.

Fit for a king: the Jordaens honeymoon suite in Hotel le Dixseptième

DELUXE

Conrad

The best address in Brussels for shopaholics is this opulent Conrad on Ave Louise. While it has all the expected facilities (including a decent indoor pool), fashionistas might find themselves mentally (or perhaps literally!) trying to get the somewhat fussy colour schemes and patterns in the room to make sense.

☎ 02 542 42 42 ⌨ www .conradhotels.com ✉ Ave Louise 71, Ixelles Ⓜ Louise ✕ 🐾 ♿ good 🚶

Hotel Amigo (4, D6)

Easily the best address in Brussels, this stylish hotel has an impossible-to-beat location (adjacent to the Grand Place) and unmatched class and service. Renovated only a couple of years ago, its modish style and detailed touches (René Magritte prints and comic strip hero Tintin give the rooms a Belgian slant) set it apart.

☎ 02 547 47 47 ⌨ www .hotelamigo.com ✉ Rue de l'Amigo 1-3, Lower Town Ⓜ Gare Centrale 🚌 Bourse ✕ ♿ good 🚶

Hôtel Métropole (4, E2)

Having celebrated its 110th birthday in 2005, the Métropole is the city's oldest hotel. However, it's a stylistic bowerbird, with the main entrance decorated in French Renaissance style, the reception hall in Empire style and some rooms featuring Art Deco touches. While we'd probably opt for the Amigo (above), we'd still swing by

Hôtel Métropole's fancy lobby

to drink at the sumptuous Café Métropole (p43).

☎ 02 217 23 00 ⌨ www .metropolehotel.be ✉ Place de Brouckère 31, Lower Town Ⓜ De Brouckère ✕ ♿ good 🚶

Stanhope (3, F5)

Just as the area it resides in is a little restrained, so is this English-country-style hotel. While they've expanded from the original three townhouses, the older ones have that more lived-in feel, while the newer rooms carry the theme into the 21st century. While hosting high-powered guests, it has a decidedly unhurried and relaxed feel.

☎ 02 506 91 11 ⌨ www .stanhope.be ✉ Rue du Commerce 9, Upper Town Ⓜ Trône ✕ ♿ good 🚶

TOP END

Hotel Astoria (3, E2)

Built in 1909, this hotel makes your eyes pop with its early-20th-century splendour from the moment you walk in – the stained glass and Art Deco skylight are stunning. This listed monument isn't just a museum piece as it has all mod-cons (including wi-fi) and for a hotel nearly 100 years old it merely feels nicely worn-in.

☎ 02 227 05 05 ⌨ www .sofitel.com ✉ Rue Royale 103, Upper Town Ⓜ Botanique ♿ fair 🚶

Hotel Le Dixseptième (4, E6)

Situated on Brussels' first paved street (close to Grand Place), parts of the building

TOP 5 SLEEPS

- Hotel Amigo (left)
- Hotel Le Dixseptième (right)
- Hotel Astoria (above)
- Hôtel Manos Premier (p52)
- Royal Windsor Hotel (fashion rooms; p52)

that this wonderful hotel resides in date back to the 14th century. Beautifully restored, the 12 rooms at the front section are a delight.
☎ 02 517 17 17 ☐ www .ledixseptieme.be ✉ Rue de la Madeleine 25, Lower Town Ⓜ Gare Centrale (♿)

Hotel Le Plaza (3, D2)

This recently restored hotel attracts stars who know they'll be treated in the manner to which they've become accustomed. The spacious standard rooms are fine, but upgrading to a deluxe room gets you a late check out and a sumptuous breakfast thrown in. So don some sunglasses, adopt some attitude and book in under a pseudonym.
☎ 02 278 01 00 ☐ www .leplaza-brussels.be ✉ Blvd Adolphe Max 118-126 Ⓜ Rogier 🍴 (♿) good (♿)

Hôtel Manos Premier
(6, A1)

Five-star sister to nearby four-star Hôtel Manos

Stéphanie (below), this hotel is an even more relaxing and inviting address. With just 35 boutique rooms and 15 suites, decorated with Louis XV and Louis XVI period furniture, it's an intimate address with a lovely private garden, an authentic *hammam* (bathhouse) and an elegant French restaurant, Kolya.
☎ 02 537 96 82 ☐ www.manoshotel.com /premier ✉ Chaussée de Charleroi 100-106, St-Gilles Ⓜ Louise (♿)

Hôtel Manos Stéphanie

This lavishly decorated hotel close to the shopping of Ave Louise appears to have more mirrors, paintings and antiques than the Hermitage Museum. Once over the initial shock, you'll discover a welcoming and well-run hotel, with charm to spare.
☎ 02 539 02 50 ☐ www.manoshotel.com /stephanie ✉ Chaussée

de Charleroi 28, St-Gilles Ⓜ Louise (♿)

Jolly Hotel du Grand Sablon (3, D5)

You'll find this elegant, friendly, cream-coloured six-floor establishment right on the Place du Grand Sablon, home to the antique market and the perfect address for chocoholics and café-loving patrons. The rooms are stylish, all have wi-fi, and four of the hotel's floors are nonsmoking.
☎ 02 518 11 00 ☐ www .jollyhotels.com ✉ Rue Bodenbroek 2-4, Sablon Ⓜ Porte de Namur (♿)

Meliá Avenue Louise
(6, A1)

Part of the Spanish Meliá group, this hotel's position sees it fill with business folk during the week while at weekends the prices are better and the vibe more relaxed. The rooms are very comfortable.
☎ 02 535 95 00 ☐ www .solmelia.com ✉ Rue Blanche 4-6, Ixelles Ⓜ Louise (♿)

Royal Windsor Hotel
(4, E6)

While this hotel close to the Grand Place appears very old-school, three of the hotel's six floors are dedicated nonsmoking floors and 'standard' rooms, decorated in a contemporary style, are excellent value. However, the biggest surprise are the hip 'fashion rooms' that were designed by local stylists – particularly the retrofuturistic room by Marina Yee.
☎ 02 505 55 55 ☐ www .royalwindsorbrussels.com ✉ Rue Duquesnoy 5, Lower Town Ⓜ Gare Centrale 🍴 (♿) good (♿)

Hôtel Manos Stéphanie's floral façade

JEAN-BERNARD CARILLET

MIDRANGE

Atlas (4, A3)

A quiet location near Place Ste-Catherine (and Rue Antoine Dansaert shopping) is the setting for this friendly, recently renovated hotel. Some of the 88 rooms come with kitchenettes (good for families) and most rooms face onto a serene courtyard. Wi-fi is available.

☎ 02 502 60 06
🖳 www.atlas-hotel.be
✉ Rue du Vieux Marché aux Grains 30, Lower Town
Ⓜ Ste-Catherine
♿ fair ♨

B&B Guilmin (Chambres en Ville) (3, F5)

A hidden gem in a quiet corner of the Upper Town, this popular B&B has four pleasant, light-filled rooms, each decorated according to a theme such as *La Vie d'Artiste,* 'life of an artist'. Indeed, the artist-owners own works are displayed throughout the rooms.

☎ 02 512 92 90 ✉ Rue de Londres 19, Upper Town
Ⓜ Trône

B&B Phileas Fogg (3, F2)

An eccentrically decorated set of rooms is the key feature of this B&B in St-Josse – a good 15- to 20-minute walk from Grand Place. The Blue Room here is the one guests rave about, with its polished floorboards, Japanese futon and eclectic antiques, while the en-suite room will sleep a family of four.

☎ 02 217 83 38 🖳 www.phileasfogg.be ✉ Rue Van Bemmel 6, St-Josse
Ⓜ Madou ♨

Arty decorations at Comfort Art Hotel Siru

Comfort Art Hotel Siru (3, D1)

While this idiosyncratic, turreted building (a hotel since 1932) is spoilt by the 'Comfort' hotel signs, this still can't ruin the interior where the rooms and public areas feature contemporary art works. All the rooms here are individually decorated, going a long way to make up for the snug size of most of the rooms.

☎ 02 203 35 80 🖳 www.comforthotelsiru.com ✉ Place Rogier 1, St-Josse
Ⓜ Rogier

Hotel Arlequin (4, D4)

This decent three-star hotel serves up 92 refurbished rooms a short stroll from the Grand Place and several clubs. While the rooms are pleasant, they're nondescript (but have wi-fi), however the breakfast room has alluring views over the city's rooftops.

☎ 02 514 16 15 🖳 www.arlequin.be ✉ Rue de la Fourche 17-19, Lower Town
Ⓜ De Brouckère

Hotel du Congrès (3, F3)

At a pleasant 10-minute walk down to the centre of town, this hotel, situated in four renovated townhouses, is fresh, sleek and comfortable. It's a smartly designed hotel (apart from the tiny TVs), with a lovely breakfast room and wi-fi.

☎ 02 217 18 90 🖳 www.hotelducongres.be ✉ Rue du Congrès 42, Madou
Ⓜ Madou

Hotel Le Dôme (3, D2)

While the Art Nouveau façade of this building is wonderful, nothing here matches it for elegance. The disappointment continues if you opt for the second building, a few doors down, so book a room in the original – preferably an atmospheric corner room. Well-equipped for the price, it's handy to the shopping of Rue Neuve.

☎ 02 218 06 80 🖳 www.hotel-le-dome.be ✉ Blvd du Jardin Botanique 9-12-13, Lower Town Ⓜ Rogier ♨

Hotel Mozart (4, E6)

No prizes for guessing what the soundtrack to this charming 50-room hotel is. Just a baton wave away from the Grand Place, don't be fooled by it's underwhelming exterior. The salmon-coloured rooms and corridors are antique-filled wonders and while the single rooms are snug, couples should go for the executive rooms which are bigger than the standard twins.

☎ 02 502 66 61 🖳 www .hotel-mozart.be ✉ Rue du Marché aux Fromages 23, Lower Town Ⓜ Gare Centrale ⏷

Hotel Noga

This excellent midrange choice is situated in a quiet street of the Ste-Catherine quarter, with very friendly service and a wonderful, idiosyncratically decorated interior. While the rooms are simpler than the richly decorated public areas, they are spotless and there's a billiards room, wi-fi, and a great little library of travel guides and novels.

☎ 02 218 67 63 🖳 www .nogahotel.com ✉ Rue du Béguinage 38, Lower Town Ⓜ Ste-Catherine ⏷

Hôtel Saint Michel

(4, D5)

It goes without saying that if you book a room here – the only hotel right on Grand Place – you must get a Place-facing room. While it's a well-run hotel in the exquisite Maison des Ducs

de Brabant, it's not as ornate as you might expect, but the views of the Place and its camera-snapping visitors are priceless.

☎ 02 511 09 56 🖳 www .hotelsaintmichel.be ✉ Grand Place 15, Lower Town Ⓜ De Brouckère ⏷ Bourse ⏷

BUDGET

Hôtel à la Grande Cloche (3, C4)

If you're looking for something away from madding crowds in the centre of town, this venerable hotel on quiet Place Rouppe, might just be your thing. Its location (an interesting 10 minutes' walk from the Grand Place) means that you get great value for money in the refurbished, decent-sized rooms, and the good

service adds to the relaxed vibe.

☎ 02 512 61 40 🖳 www .hotelgrandecloche.com ✉ Place Rouppe 10, Marolles Ⓜ Gare du Midi ⏷ Anneessens

Hôtel Galia (3, C5)

With views over the famous sprawling Marolles flea market (7am to 2pm daily), this simple hotel is certainly located in an atmospheric spot. Recently expanded, the comic-adorned hotel is clean, well-maintained and good value.

☎ 02 502 42 43 🖳 www .hotelgalia.com ✉ Place du Jeu de Balle 15-16, Marolles Ⓜ Porte de Hal

Sleep Well (3, D2)

This large, well-run hostel (and now hotel) has a central location close to Place des Martyrs. While there are dorm-style rooms (with lock-out from 11am to 3pm), the newer 'Sleep Well Star Rooms' have their own facilities and no lock-out. It's your classic busy hostel, with people from all walks and a great place to meet other travellers.

☎ 02 218 50 50 🖳 www .sleepwell.be ✉ Rue du Damier 23, Lower Town Ⓜ Rogier ⏷ good

JEAN-BERNARD CARILLET

Hotel Mozart's (p53) lounge

HISTORY

Although present-day Brussels was settled by Neolithic peoples from around 2250 BC, the name 'Belgium' came from a Celtic tribe, the Belgae, who lived here around 900 BC until Caesar arrived in 52 BC bringing Belgium under Roman rule. The Romans spent some 500 years here before being booted out by Germanic Franks, but it wasn't until 695 when bishop St-Géry erected a chapel on an island in swampy River Senne (Zenne) that a settlement called Bruocsella (from *bruoc* for swamp and *sella* for dwelling) sprang up. It wasn't until 977 when emperor Otto II gave Charles, banished son of France's King Louis IV Charles, the small St-Géry castle, that Brussels was truly born.

When French king Charlemagne conquered Belgium, he divided his empire among his counts, with their governing areas in Belgium corresponding roughly to the divide that exists today between French-speaking Wallonia and Flemish-speaking Flanders.

Flanders developed first with it feudal counts exerting their influence in the late 9th century by building fortresses in Ghent and Bruges, while Brussels' Coudenberg palace (and following it a defensive wall) wasn't constructed until the 11th century. Brussels outgrew its walls by the 14th century, when a second pentagon-shaped wall was built, twice as long as the first.

French king Philip the Good reigned partly from Brussels in the 15th century, building the Grand Place and bringing culture to the city, although the 16th century brought the Reformation, a Protestant rethink of Catholic edicts, resulting in Low Country revolts against Spanish Catholic rule. When the Spanish made Brussels capital of the Spanish

JOHN ELK III

GUILDS
The guildhouses you'll see around Belgium (generally built around the 16th century) are the headquarters of trades- and craftsmen, who formed these guilds to set standards for their particular trade. Principally run by wealthy families, these guilds also wielded political power and, in some stages of history in Belgium, ruled at a local level.

ROYAL REVERSAL

While Léopold II's ambition and cruelty is legendary (his late-19th-century reign manifested in the Congo's exploitation and monumental construction in Brussels), Albert I was more likable. Ruling from 1909, he commanded the Belgian army during WWI, virtually leading the Allied offensive and recapturing the country's coastline in 1918. Léopold III, in contrast, surrendered Belgium when Germany invaded in WWII and, with the government exiled in London, the Jewish population was wiped out. Léopold III abdicated in 1950, to be replaced by son, Baudouin, who gave the Congo independence in 1959 and was popular for his fair treatment of Walloons and Flemish. Baudouin died in 1993 and the current king is another likable Albert, the second.

Netherlands in 1585, more pan-European bloodshed followed, including the city's 36-hour bombardment by Marshal De Villeroy (acting under orders of Louis XIV) in August 1695, which levelled the Grand Place (see boxed text, p8).

In the 18th century the ruling Austrian Habsburgs fostered the city's development and were responsible for many architectural highlights. The French incorporated the area into France in 1794 until Napoleon's defeat at Waterloo in 1815, which led to the creation of the United Kingdom of the Netherlands, incorporating present-day Netherlands, Belgium and Luxembourg, until King William I tried to make Dutch the national language 15 years later, and the French- and Flemish-speaking Belgians sent them home.

Belgian independence was recognised in January 1831 at the Conference of London, and on 21 July Léopold was made king. The constitution was drawn up in French, the language of the elite,

King Baudouin in front of Cathédrale des Sts Michel & Gudules (p13)

and it took another 70 years before the Dutch tongue was acknowledged as Belgium's 'second' language, fuelling cultural tensions. These persisted until 1962 when the regions of Flanders, Wallonia and bilingual Brussels were created, forming a linguistic divide.

GOVERNMENT, POLITICS & ECONOMY

A constitutional hereditary monarchy, Belgium is led by King Albert II and a parliament consisting of a Senate and Chamber of Representatives, which have responsibility for national legislation, policy, finance, defence and foreign affairs. The government was decentralised in 1993 resulting in three regional governments representing the Dutch- and French-speaking communities (Flanders and Wallonia respectively) and the Brussels Capital Region, a significant step on a long path of constitutional reform that started in the 1960s, when the Dutch, French and German-speaking communities began demanding linguistic, territorial and cultural autonomy.

While Brussels is Belgium's capital, it's also capital of the Flemish region and the Ardennes town of Namur is the seat of the Walloon regional government. Just to add another bureaucratic layer, Brussels was officially designated the European capital in 1993 and is home to the European Commission (since 1958); NATO (since 1967), the policy-making executive branch of the EU; the publicly elected European Parliament, which funds and keeps an eye on the Commission; and the Council of Ministers, which ratifies legislation proposed by the Commissioners.

Belgium's political scene has long been dominated by the (Catholic) Christian Democrats, Socialists and Liberals, though support for greens (Agalev in Flanders, Ecolo in Wallonia) is increasing. Belgium was governed throughout the 1990s by an ever-changing coalition headed by Christian Democrat Jean-Luc Dehaene, during which time political scandals eroded confidence in them. In 1999 Belgium opted for an unusual coalition of Liberals, Socialists and Greens, headed by Guy Verhofstadt, the first Liberal prime minister in 50 years.

In the 2003 national elections, the Socialists and Liberals won two-thirds of the parliamentary seats, renewing their coalition, with Verhofstadt as leader and this is likely to remain so until the next general election in 2007. To everyone's concern, the Vlaams Blok, campaigning on a platform of 'Our Own People First', won 20% of the popular vote in Flanders and 10% of the national vote, although it's since been banned (see p93).

Belgium was Europe's first country to industrialise and its main growth industries include textiles, machinery, diamonds, engineering and financial services. Its economic prosperity has swung from one language community to the other over the centuries, starting with Flanders' medieval textile wealth, then Wallonia's coal, iron and steel industries (which declined in the 1950s and '60s), with Flanders becoming the country's economic powerhouse. The resulting Flemish assertiveness and Wallonian insecurity was a major imperative for the creation of the 'linguistic divide'.

Brussels' World Trade Centre

Flanders remains the dominant economic force, especially in high-tech industries, and is the third most advanced in the EU.

With one of the most integrated and open economies in Europe, the Belgian economy is getting healthier with a strong GDP helped by domestic and foreign demand, falling inflation and public debt slowly reducing, although national unemployment is still high at 8.5%.

SOCIETY & CULTURE

Belgium's linguistically and culturally divided population of nearly 11 million people is split between Dutch-speaking Flanders (Vlaanderen in Dutch) in the north with 60% of the population, French-speaking Wallonia (la Wallonie in French) in the south with 27%, and the German-speaking eastern cantons in Belgium's far east, comprising 13% of the population. It's important to note that the Dutch spoken by the Flemish is the Flemish dialect of Dutch and many Flemish prefer if you call the language Flemish.

Bilingual Brussels (technically in Flanders, but dominated by French speakers) has a multicultural population of one million that includes many other European nationalities, Moroccans, Turks and Africans (mainly immigrants from the former Belgian Congo). Roughly three-quarters of Belgians are Catholic, with Protestants, Jews and Muslims making up the rest.

The Bruxellois can be both reserved and exceedingly friendly, confident yet modest, efficient yet relaxed, stern and cheeky and love creating rules only to then break them. They have a love of life that seems to simultaneously embrace anything that is adventurous and new, yet have a fear of change and losing their traditions.

ARTS
Architecture

Brussels' architectural highlights span everything from Victor Horta's Art Nouveau masterpieces to medieval ecclesiastical achievements and the World Heritage–listed Grand Place. The Romanesque edifices of the Middle Ages are characterised by columns and semicircular arches, progressing to pointed Gothic arches. A wonderful example of the dominant Brabant Gothic style of the 15th century is the beautiful symmetry of the Hôtel de Ville (p21), but this pales against the exuberant ornateness of some of the baroque architecture, and the guildhalls on the Grand Place (levelled in 1695, see boxed text, p8) are a fine example of the Flemish Renaissance style.

Eighteenth-century Austrian rule left the city with elegant neoclassical buildings, on display around Place Royale, which was followed by postindependence extravagance and neo-Renaissance constructions such as the Galeries

JEAN-BERNARD CARILLET

Magnificent Grand Place at an angle (p8)

BELGIAN ARTISTS – CRASH COURSE

- Jan Van Eyck – an innovator whose greatest achievements were portraits, particularly of happily married couples and angelic women
- Pieter Paul Rubens – 'Rubenesque' was coined after his voluptuous women
- Paul Delvaux – painted nude women in absurd dream-like settings
- René Magritte – painted the most surreal dreamscapes of them all (image below)
- Panamarenko – specialises in space ships!

Royales St-Hubert and Léopold II's Palais de Justice (p22). After Art Nouveau, exemplified by Victor Horta, came the cool, clean lines of Art Deco, the best example being the Musée David et Alice van Buuren (p20). The last half of the 20th century brought a grab bag of architecture, including the futuristic Atomium (p21) and the postmodern mess of the EU area.

Painting & Sculpture

Flemish primitives of the 15th-century Rogier Van de Weyden, Dirk Bouts, Hans Memling, and Jan Van Eyck produced rich works that can be seen around Belgium. One of the most influential artists was Hieronymus Bosch, with his extraordinary allegories. The greatest 16th-century artist was Pieter Bruegel the Elder, who painted peasant life. Pieter Paul Rubens produced more than 2000 artworks and nurtured baroque artists, such as Antoon Van Dyck and Jacob Jordaens. The 19th century brought the monumental canvases of Antoine Wiertz,

The one-and-only Jan Van Eyck

the bronze sculptures of Constantin Meunier, and James Ensor's vivid portraits, while 20th-century greats included landscapist Rik Wouters and dreamy surrealists such as René Magritte and Paul Delvaux, as well as wacky Panamarenko.

Literature

Belgium's low-key literary history began more or less in the 18th century, when Willem Verhoeven and Jan Baptist Verlooy reacted to the French influence in literature with their Flemish-inspired styles. The following century's writings were romantic, with close links to the revival in Flemish nationalist feelings, and works such as Hendrik Conscience's 1838 novel *De Leeuw van Vlaanderen (The Lion of Flanders)* while Flemish poet Guido Gezelle revived poetry with his popular *The Evening* and the *Rose*. Popular 20th-century writers include Hugo Claus, who attracted international interest with *Het Verdriet van België (The Sorrow of Belgium)* in 1983, while arguably the most famous writer is the prolific (French-resident) Georges Simenon, who wrote detective stories centred on Inspector Maigret. The most interesting Belgian authors around now are two young women: Anne Provoost, whose captivating *Falling* has won a number of awards, and Japanese-born Amélie Nothomb, who has a cult following in France and writes elegant, imaginative and semi-autobiographical novels, such as *Fear and Trembling* (1999).

Music

Whenever Belgium has experienced success on the music scene, it's been meteoric. It all started with medieval folk songs and their marvellous carillons (bells attached to town clocks) – Belgium now has a renowned campanology school near the town of Mechelen. Composer André-Modeste Grétry achieved fame as the 17th-century father of comic opera, and late-19th-century opera in Brussels was deservedly popular too. These achievements were topped in the 20th century by Adolphe Sax's invention of the saxophone, renowned jazz guitarist Django Reinhardt and harmonica player Toots Thielemans, and singer Jacques Brel's extraordinary rise in French show business. In more recent years, Belgium has been the home of house, techno and trance with its DJs and musicians (such as 2ManyDJs/Soulwax) making their mark on the international club scene.

JEAN-BERNARD CARILLET

A DJ's magic hands at Fuse (p46)

Picture postcard pretty Bruges (Brugge in Flemish, Bruges in French) is Belgium's most popular destination. And while this medieval wonder deserves its more than two million visitors a year, sometimes during summer you may wonder whether they're all here at once.

No matter how crowded the town is when you visit, you can't help but be awe-struck at the Markt, with its massive Belfort rising 83m in the square and soundtrack provided by the clip-clop of the horse-drawn carriages transporting transfixed tourists around the sights. In the warmer months, a beer at one of the cafés is an obligation. Just a block or so away, the Burg, the former seat of the counts of Flanders is often less crowded but arguably no less impressive.

Cobbled street scene in Bruges

Equally as impressive is the city's art collection such as that of the Groeningemuseum, with its prized collection of Flemish primitives. For those more interested in elbow bending than canvas stretching, De Halve Maan, a brewery operating since 1856, offers a brewery tour and a tasting of their Brugse Zot beer. For those interested in picking up some Belgian lace, you can watch it being hand-made at the Kantcentrum (Lace Centre).

However, one of the best things in Bruges is just to wander around. Head down to the Begijnhof and Minnewater, where the ducks and swans glide amidst painterly surroundings. At dusk, after the day-trippers have headed off, you might just see why Bruges became so popular in the first place.

Tranquil Begijnhof (p63) at dusk

Bruges' perfectly preserved **medieval centre** is both surrounded and severed by canals, with the outer canal encircled by a ring road. The area outside this ring road is Bruges' suburbia with little to interest visitors.

The heart of Bruges' compact centre is the magnificent Markt, a lively square (gorgeous at night) lined with elegant guildhouses and busy with tourists lining up for horse and carriage rides, and the towering Belfort (belfry), with magnificent views. Adjoining the Markt is the Burg, a small elegant square surrounded by breathtaking buildings, including the Stadhuis and the Heilig-Bloedbasiliek. And from Burg you can take an atmospheric lane, the Blinde Ezelstraat (Blind Donkey Street) to access the Vismarkt (Fish Market) and pretty Huidenvettersplein. From here, along the Groenerei, and along the Dijver, are some of the most enchanting views, especially in the early evening.

In the largely pedestrianised streets surrounding the Markt and Burg are scores of restaurants, cafés, pubs, shops and museums, dotted with pretty squares, and while the streets aren't always quiet, they're always walkable, unlike Ghent's thoroughfares ruled by bikes – just look out for the horses and carriages, although fortunately you'll always hear the clip-clop first.

The main shopping streets in Bruges are Wollestraat and Kate-lijnestraat for regional products (chocolates, beer and lace) and souvenirs, Braambergstraat for art galleries and antiques, Steenstraat for high street brands, and Geldmuntstraat for Belgian designers. West of here is the Concertgebouw and tourist office, and southwest of here the railway station.

You'll find many of Bruges' museums off the Dijver, such as the Groeningemuseum and Gruuthusemuseum. A short walk south of here you'll find an atmospheric area off Walplein and the pretty Begijnhof and Minnewater. To the east of the centre is the **St-Anna** area, home to Jeruzalemkerk, along with the area north and northwest of the centre, is largely residential, but worth exploring for just that.

OFF THE BEATEN TRACK

Keen to escape the tourist crowds in Bruges? The areas north and east of the main historic centre, especially the neighbourhood of St-Anna, is largely residential, with gabled guildhouses, tiny cottages, quiet cobblestone lanes and tranquil streets – and barely a tourist in sight, especially off-season. Shut this book for a while and get lost. It's glorious!

Cobbles galore in Bruges

TERRY CARTER

Begijnhof

Enjoy a quiet stroll in the garden of this pretty Begijnhof (see box). Its modest whitewashed houses were a tranquil haven for beguines from 1245 and are still home to a small community of single women. You can walk from the canal beside the Begijnhof to a lovely tree-lined **Minnewater**.

✉ Wijngaardstraat
🕙 9am-7pm Apr-Sep, 9am-6pm Oct-Mar

Burg (1, D3)

This small square has some splendid sights. The **Heilig-Bloedbasiliek** (Basilica of the Holy Blood) has a sober 12th-century Romanesque lower chapel and lavish upper chapel housing

Check it out at the Groeningemuseum

a relic of Christ's blood, brought here by Crusaders between 1150 and 1200 and venerated each day. The **Stadhuis**, Belgium's oldest town hall (built 1376–1420), has a Gotische Zaal (Gothic Hall) with a sumptuous carved ceiling and magnificent murals depicting Flanders' glorious past.

☎ 050 44 87 11 🕙 Basilica 9.30-11.50am & 2-5.50pm

Apr-Sep, 10-11.50am & 2-3.50pm Oct-Mar; Gotische Zaal 9.30am-5pm Tue-Sun
€ Gotische Zaal €2.50/free/1.50

De Halve Maan

Operating since 1856, the cosy De Halve Maan, brewer of delicious Brugse Zot beer, is the only family brewery still running in the town centre. While you'll have a few laughs on the 45-minute tour through the brewery, you may not always get to see everything well as it can get very crowded.

☎ 050 33 26 97 ✉ Walplein 26 🕙 11am-4pm Apr-Oct, 11am & 3pm Nov-Mar € €4.50 incl a glass of Brugse Zot

Groeningemuseum (1, D5)

While this may house one of the most sublime collections of Flemish medieval painting, unfortunately a misjudged renovation has visitors wondering why they're viewing art while standing on a dirty white tiled floor. Focus instead on the fantastic Hieronymus Bosch triptych *The Last Judgement* and the works of Jan Van Eyck.

☎ 050 44 87 43 ✉ Dijver 12 🕙 9.30am-5pm Tue-Sun € €8/free/6

THE BEGIJNEN & BEGIJNHOVEN

The *begijnen* (or beguines) were a Catholic order of single and widowed women who, following the loss of men to the Crusades, joined together for support. They took vows of chastity and obedience to God, but refused to live in poverty, working together to make a living producing textiles or getting paid to pray for their benefactors. The *begijnhoven* (or *beguinages*) were their sanctuaries, clusters of cottages around central gardens, surrounded by protective walls. There were around 1500 beguines in Belgium at the beginning of the 20th century, although only 22 exist now, with one of the best preserved in Bruges.

Memlingmuseum

Gruuthusemuseum
(1, C5)
Occupying the 15th-century palace of the Lords of Gruuthuse who got rich through a tax on *gruut* (an ingredient used for brewing beer), the Gruuthusemuseum has a wonderful collection of decorative and applied arts, musical instruments and weapons. Nearby, the **Arentshuis** (Dijver 16; admission €2.50/ free/1.50) exhibits paintings by Bruges artist Frank Brangwyn (1867–1956).
☎ 050 44 87 43 ✉ Dijver 17 ☺ 9.30am-5pm Tue-Sun € €6/free/4

Jeruzalemkerk
This 15th-century Church of the Holy Sepulchre is, oddly enough, a replica of the one in Jerusalem. Stranger yet is its macabre altarpiece. The adjoining **Kantcentrum** (Lace Centre) has a museum and workshop where women make lace – watch them and you'll develop an immense appreciation of lace that you didn't realise was possible!
☎ 050 33 00 72 ✉ Peperstraat 3 ☺ 10am-noon & 2-6pm Mon-Fri, 10am-noon

& 2-5pm Sat € €2.50/ free/1.50

Markt (1, C3)
Lively Markt square is always busy, with locals shopping at the morning market, tourists embarking on horse-drawn carriage tours and drunk visitors celebrating hen and stag nights. Divert your attention from this to admire the gabled medieval buildings and the Unesco World Heritage listed **Belfort** (belfry), which, once you climb the 366 steps, has great views.
€ €5/2.50 ☺ Belfort 9.30am-5pm Tue-Sun, last tickets 4.15pm

Memlingmuseum (1, C6)
Home to masterpieces by Hans Memling (1440–94) and other painters from his time, the museum occupies the restored 12th-century St-Janshospitaal. While the small collection is wonderful, especially the St-Ursula Shrine, this is unfortunately another museum that's suffered from an ill-conceived renovation.
☎ 050 44 87 43 ✉ Mariastraat 38 ☺ 9.30am-5pm Tue-Sun € €8/free/5

Museum voor Volkskunde
This fascinating Folklore Museum, occupying a row

of restored 17th-century *godshuizen* (almshouses built by wealthy philanthropists for the poor), has some delightful exhibits, including a classroom, tailor's, sweet shop, milliner's and lacemaker's shop.
☎ 050 44 87 43 ✉ Rolweg 40 ☺ 9.30am-5pm Tue-Sun € €3/free/2

Onze-Lieve-Vrouwekerk
(1, C6)
Surprisingly, the highlight of the austere gothic Church of Our Lady is a small marble statue of Michelangelo's Madonna brought here by a Bruges merchant during the Renaissance and the only piece by Michelangelo to ever leave Italy.
✉ Mariastraat ☺ 9.30am-12.30pm & 1.30-5pm Tue-Sat, 1.30-5pm Sun

St-Salvatorskathedraal
(1, B5)
The 13th-century St Saviour's Cathedral is the city's oldest church. Recently renovated, its exterior with its 99m neo-Romanesque tower is much more impressive than the bare interior.
✉ Steenstraat ☺ 2-5.45pm Mon, 9am-noon & 2-5.45pm Tue-Fri, 9am-noon & 2-3.30pm Sat, 9-10.15am & 2-5.45pm Sun

Get your flowers on the Markt on market day

Bubbles & Co (1, D4)
Popular with English tourists who leave here with bags full of scented candles and soaps, from mimosa to algae, and Christmas pudding to rhubarb and custard! Tshe *chocolate chaude pralinés de savon* look remarkably like real chocolates – smell them to see why they're so popular. We love the candles handmade by a local grandfather.
☎ 050 615 271 ✉ Wolle-straat 21 ☼ 10am-12.30pm & 2-6pm

Brugs Bierhuis (1, B3)
The only beer shop focusing on beer (and a small range of *jenevers*), without the tacky souvenirs others sell. You'll find hundreds of different types of Belgian beers, including Bruges beers, Abbey Ales, Westmalle and Trappist Tripel, and great gift packs with matching glasses. Go for the Belgian Beer Tour with 16 bottles of different beers!
☎ 050 34 63 08 ✉ Geld-muntstraat 22 ☼ 10am-6.30pm Mon-Sat, 2-6pm Sun

Callebert (1, D3)
Callebert specialises in contemporary European design across a range of home prod-

ucts. Stelton's Arne Jacobsen stainless steel teapot or a Philippe Starck kitchen knife set may fit snugly in the suitcase, but you might have trouble explaining the Vitra Eames chairs or a Belgian-designed Quinze and Milan pouf to customs.
☎ 050 33 50 61 ✉ Wolle-straat 25 ☼ 10am-noon & 2-6pm Tue-Sat, 3-6pm Sun & Mon

De Reyghere Reisboekhandel (1, C3)
This specialised travel bookshop stocks a great range of books on Bruges and Belgium, guides (including Lonely Planet) and travelogues, in English, Dutch and French. Next door, their sister store has general fiction and nonfiction, plus English newspapers.
☎ 050 49 12 29 ✉ Markt 13 ☼ 9.30am-12.30pm & 1.30-6pm Mon-Sat

De Striep
The place to come for comics in Bruges, De Striep has a comprehensive collection in Dutch, French and English. Try to get hold of Thibaut Vandorselaer's wonderful illustrated historical guide to the city, *Bruges Through*

Comic Strips: A Journey of Discovery.
☎ 050 33 71 12 ✉ Kate-lijnestraat 42 ☼ 10am-12.30pm & 1.30-7pm Tue-Sat, 2-6pm Sun

Diksmuids Boterhuis (1, B3)
In the Willems family for 43 years, this old-fashioned cheese shop with enticing window displays was started by the father of the current owner, a lovely chatty woman with a passion for fine cheeses, salamis, hams, pâtés, mustards and relishes.
☎ 050 33 32 43 ✉ Geld-muntstraat 23 ☼ 9am-1pm & 2-7pm Mon-Sat

Galler (1, C4)
While Jean Galler grew up in his grandfather's chocolate shop, his own company is only 20 years old. A youthful willingness to experiment is what accounts for its innovative chocolates (tea or curry perhaps?) and chic orange and black packaging. We love their wine and chocolate gift sets.
☎ 050 61 20 62 ✉ Steen-straat 5 ☼ 9am-1pm & 2-7pm Mon-Sat

L'Héroïne (1, B4)
This stylish understated store specialises in women's (and some men's) clothing, jewellery and accessories by brilliant Belgian designers Dries Van Noten, Dirk Bikkembergs, Anna Heylen, AF Vandevorst, Kaat Tilley and milliner Christophe Coppens.
☎ 050 33 56 57 ✉ Noord-zandstraat 32 ☼ 10am-6.30pm Mon-Sat

Careful with those *tripels*!

BOBBIN IN BRUGES

Bruges is big on lace (*kant* in Flemish or *dentelle* in French), as you would have noticed from the many lace shops between the Markt and Burg. Bobbin lace *(kloskant)* is the type made in and said to have originated in Bruges, and is created by women who speedily and meticulously move fine threads around pins using bobbins, following patterns that have been in their family for generations. Watch the women at work at the Kantcentrum (p64), and to ensure you're buying the genuine article (most lace sold in Bruges is machine-made from Taiwan) shop at 't Apostelientje (right).

Olivier Strelli (1, B3 & C3)
Belgium's most-loved designer of stylish men's and women's fashion is best known for creating looks combining bold colour, rich textures and detailed prints, with, say, a crushed linen or beautifully cut pin-striped suit. While the women's collections are pretty and feminine, the men's is generally more adventurous.
☎ men's 050 33 26 75, women's 050 34 38 37
✉ men's Geldmuntstraat

19, women's Eiermarkt 3
🕑 10am-12.30pm & 1.30pm-6.30pm Mon-Sat

Rombaux (1, E3)
This large old-fashioned music store, specialising in classical music, jazz, world music, folk and Flemish music, is the kind of place you can browse for hours. They have an excellent range of jazz and opera DVDs, sheet music and musical instruments.
☎ 050 33 25 75
✉ Mallebergplaats 13

🕑 9am -12.30pm Mon-Fri & 9-6pm Saturday

't Apostelientje
This lovely lace shop, across from Jerusalem Church and its awe-inspiring (yes, really!) lace museum (p64) has an expansive range of garments and gifts made from authentic handmade Bruges lace. The owners are experts so you can be sure you're getting the real weave.
☎ 050 33 78 60
✉ Balstraat 11
🕑 9.30am-6pm Mon-Sat & 10am-1pm Sun

Zazou (1, C3)
Crammed on weekends with women crowding the counter to try on funky silver jewellery and vibrant accessories sourced from independent European designers. If you like what you see here, head across the pedestrian mall to Swing Swing Zazou, specialising in colourful beaded jewellery and chunky wooden necklaces.
☎ 050 33 46 27
✉ St-Amandsstraat 19 & 20
🕑 10am-12.30pm & 2-6.30pm Mon-Sat

Olivier Strelli's stylish fashion

Bistro de Eetkamer
(1, D4)
Modern Belgian €€€
This petite restaurant is one of Bruges' more impressive eateries. The seasonal menu is mainly Belgian-based but the chefs here give it a satisfying modern twist. With only a few tables and plenty of local business be sure to book ahead.
☎ 050 33 78 86
✉ Eekhoutstraat 6
🕑 noon-2pm & 6.30-10pm Fri-Tue

Cafédraal (1, B5)
Seafood €€
A great restaurant/bar that serves up excellent seafood in an eclectically decorated set of spaces. While you're trying to figure out how it manages to be both hip and homely at once, order the oysters and bouillabaisse. Kitchen's open late too, so it's a good post-9pm choice in a town that's light on late-night eating.
☎ 050 34 08 45 🖥 www .cafedraal.be in Dutch & French ✉ Zilverstraat 38
🕑 noon-3pm & 6-11pm Mon-Sat

Christophe (1, E6)
Bistro €€€
If you've been sampling the local brews and forgot to have dinner, finding a decent feed in Bruges after 9pm can be a challenge – however Christophe comes to the rescue. It's a great little restaurant serving up a mix of French and Belgian seasonal specials late into the night – but it gets busy, so call before heading over.
☎ 050 34 48 92 🖥 www .christophe-brugge.be

When too much whipped cream is not enough

DOUG MCKINLAY

✉ Garenmarkt 34 🕑 7pm-2am Thu-Mon

De Karmeliet (1, F3)
French €€€€
Happily ensconced in the rarefied atmosphere of Michelin's thrice-starred establishments, De Karmeliet delivers what Michelin reviewers have a fondness for: supercilious waiters, a wine list only a bodybuilder could manage to lift and more courses than the average mortal eats in a week. There are several different menus of fussily presented perfection here, but while the food *is* fantastic, it's a rather soulless affair.
☎ 050 33 82 59 🖥 www .dekarmeliet.be ✉ Lange-straat 19 🕑 noon-2pm Tue-Sun, 7-9.30pm Tue-Sat

De Koetse (1, C5)
Belgian €€
While the tourists get their wallets lightened on the Markt, locals head here when they want some mussels or a great steak along with friendly service. Try favourites such as the mussels with beer and cream or for the real culinary adventurers eel in spinach sauce awaits. Less courageous souls should try the shrimp croquettes and the grilled beef – both excellent.
☎ 050 33 76 80 🖥 www .dekoetse-brugge.be
✉ Oude Burg 31 🕑 noon-2.30pm & 6-10pm Fri-Wed

De Stove (1, C4)
Belgian €€
While this small family-run restaurant is well-known for its intimate atmosphere, we love the fact that they do everything on the premises except catch the daily fresh fish. The monthly menu, which takes advantage of seasonal produce, is a great choice and the wine list thankfully features some New World wines.
☎ 050 33 78 35 🖥 www .restaurantdestove.be

✉ Kleine St-Amandsstraat 4 🕑 noon-2pm & 6.30-9.30pm Fri-Tue

Den Dyver (1, D4)
Belgian €€
Beer aficionados will love this refined eatery as all the dishes are cooked in beer and you're presented with the same beer to accompany the dish, demonstrating the incredible breadth of flavours that beer has to offer. There's a good range of set menus as well as à la carte and the restaurant has a great ambiance.
☎ 050 33 60 69
🖳 www.dendyver.be
✉ Dijver 5 🕑 noon-2pm & 6.30-9pm, closed Wed & lunch Thu

Den Gouden Karpel (1, E4)
Seafood brasserie €€
It's no surprise that this long-standing seafood brasserie serves up the freshest seafood around given its location near the fish market. It's a great place to try local specialities such as *waterzooi* (a creamy stew) of fish or any of the eel dishes – the less daring can

stick to dishes such as the bouillabaisse.
☎ 050 33 34 94
🖳 www.dengoudenkarpel .be ✉ Huidenvettersplein 4 🕑 noon-2pm & 6-10pm closed Mon & dinner Sun

Gran Kaffee De Passage (1, A5)
Brasserie €
This casual, funky and slightly grungy café has one of the best atmospheres in town. With a mix of regulars, travellers and those staying at the hostel and hotel (p73), its candle-lit interior has a vibe that's unique in town. Less than unique (but very satisfying) is the short menu of hearty dishes such as lasagne and

lamb chops – both highly recommended.
☎ 050 34 02 32
🖳 www.passagebruges .com ✉ Dweersstraat 26-28 🕑 6-11pm (closes midnight) Ⓥ

Heer Halewyn
French €€
This intimate restaurant, housed in a red brick building, is a favourite for its good wine selection and tasty grills. The short menu features some great dishes and the meat – cooked on a open fire – is what locals come here for. Brilliant on a cold Bruges night.
☎ 050 33 92 61 ✉ Walplein 10 🕑 6.30-10pm Wed-Sun

Het Dagelijks Brood (1, D3)
Bakery/café €
The Bruges branch of this national bakery and tearoom is perfect for a quick snack if you're busy trying to do all the sights in one day. The long communal table makes for a convivial atmosphere and the excellent sandwiches are made with the freshest bread imaginable.
☎ 050 33 60 50 ✉ Philipstockstraat 21 🕑 8am-6pm Wed-Mon

JEAN-BERNARD CARILLET

TERRY CARTER

L'Intermede (1, A4)
French €€
This tiny restaurant is a popular one with locals who come for the simple French bistro fare. A good choice for a romantic dinner.
☎ 050 33 16 74 ✉ Wulf-hagestraat 3 🕑 noon-2pm & 6-10pm Tue-Sat

Rock Fort (1, F3)
French/Belgian €€€
This minimiracle of a restaurant was the talk of the town when it first opened a couple of years ago. The two chefs here (Peter Laloo and Hermes Vanliefde) have a way of working French, Italian and Belgian staples (that don't always excite when read on the menu)

JEAN-BERNARD CARILLET

into shapes and flavours that lift it beyond being just a 'fusion' restaurant. Today their reputation is such that bookings can be hard to come by. If you miss out, you can always try their Barsalon (p70) next door.
☎ 050 33 41 13 🖳 www .rock-fort.be in Dutch ✉ Langestraat 15-17 🕑 noon-2.30pm & 6.30pm-11pm Tue-Sat

Saint Amour ('t Voermanshuys) (1, C4)
French €€€
This atmospheric vaulted cellar restaurant is a step back into the past to either the late 1500s – when the cellar was built – or the late 1970s – when the restaurant appears to have been last decorated. The food however, makes a convincing effort to transcend. Dishes such as cuckoo stuffed with lobster and truffles and crispy pancetta sound headed for catastrophe, but are delicious and the romantic setting is perfect for courageous culinary couples.
☎ 050 33 71 72 🖳 www.saint-amour.be ✉ Oude Burg 14 🕑 noon-2.30pm & 6-10pm Wed-Sun

Sans Cravate
Modern Belgian €€€
Before earning its first star from Michelin in 2006, Sans Cravate was whispered about by local foodies as yet another fantastic eatery along Langestraat – and they were right. The food is inventive, with the seafood dishes really shining – the sea bass with mussels is sublime. The service, however, was anything but, managing to be both clumsy and condescending.
☎ 050 67 83 10 ✉ Lange-straat 159 🕑 noon-2pm & 7-9.30pm, closed Sun, Mon & lunch Sat

Tanuki
Japanese €€
Minimalist, cute and classic, Tanuki is the only Japanese restaurant of note in town – and it's a good one. For lunch you could try the bento box or the sushi and sashimi sets (great value) and for dinner during winter they do plenty of warming dishes such as shabu-shabu in addition to the all-year-round noodles.
☎ 050 34 75 12 🖳 www.tanuki.be ✉ Oude Gentweg 1 🕑 noon-2pm & 6.30-9.30pm Wed-Sun

Barsalon (1, F2)
Adjoining Rock Fort (p69)
restaurant is a groovy
cocktail and wine bar playing
cool music and serving up
tasty 'teasers' – tapas-style
snacks such as 'pizza tortilla'
and sashimi – to soak up
the spirits. Frustratingly, it's
closed weekends.
☎ 050 61 09 38
✉ Langestraat 15-17
☷ noon-2.30pm & 5pm-
1am Mon-Thu, noon-2am Fri

Café Vlissinghe (1, F1)
The atmospheric interior
of Bruges' oldest pub,
established in 1515, hasn't
changed much since it
opened (note the ornate
wooden bar). Once fre-
quented by artists such as
Van Dyck (his chair's still
here), the tavern attracts
more tourists than locals
these days. There's a shady
garden for drinking beer and
playing *boules*.
☎ 050 34 37 37
✉ Blekersstraat 2
☷ 11am-midnight
Wed-Sat, 11am-7pm Sun

Concertgebouw (1, A6)
Catch a wide range of
cultural events in this controversial concert space and
cultural centre on the edge
of the town centre, with
everything from baroque
orchestras, choirs, piano
recitals, folk music and ballet
to innovative performances
combining opera and film,
and a growing contemporary
art collection.
☎ info 050 47 69 99, tickets
070 22 33 02 ▯ www.con
certgebouw.be ✉ 't Zand 34
☷ box office 10am-6pm
Mon-Fri, 10am-1pm Sat &
1hr before performance

BRUGES FESTS
- Cactusfestival (www.cactusmusic.be in Dutch) –
  three-day world music festival in July
- Cinema Novo Film Festival (www.cinemanovo
  .be) – 10-day festival of third world film in March
- Festival Musica Antiqua (www.musica-antiqua.com) –
  week-long music festival in February
- Heilig-Bloedprocessie – Bruges' most famous annual
  procession of a relic of Christ's blood through the city
  on Ascension Day in May

Flags are raised for the Heilig-Bloedprocessie

Cultuurcentrum (1, C2)
An innovative programme of
contemporary global dance,
theatre, music, comedy and
spoken-word, often incorporating video, live music and
electronica, can be seen at
Stadsschouwburg, Concert-
gebouw and several other
locations. Performances
could be in Dutch, French or
English, so check first.
☎ info 050 44 30 40/60,
tickets 070 22 50 05
▯ www.cultuurcentrum
brugge.be ✉ Vlamingstraat
29 ☷ box office 10am-6pm
Mon-Fri, 10am-1pm Sat

De Republiek (1, B2)
Young locals cram this arty
café-bar-club (in the same
space as Lumiere Cinema,
opposite) most evenings for
the cool DJ vibes, (occasional)
live music, cheap eats and
the buzzy atmosphere that's
lacking in many of Bruges'
bars.
☎ 050 34 02 29
✉ St-Jakobsstraat 36
☷ 11am-late

De Versteende Nacht
This dark bar, with its walls
covered in cartoons and
comics about the place, is a

popular venue for live jazz music.

☎ 050 34 32 93 ✉ Lange-straat 11 ☺ 7pm-1am Tue-Thu, 6pm-1am Fri & Sat

Est Wijnbar (1, B4)

This lively wine bar fills with chatty locals focusing on the wine (nearly 100 varieties available) and house speciality of *raclette* (melted cheese, ham, gherkins and pickled onions). They jam the place on Sunday nights to listen to live jazz, ragtime, blues and folk, from 8pm to 10.30pm.

☎ 050 33 38 39 ✉ Noord-zandstraat 34 ☺ 5pm-1am Thu, Sun & Mon, 3pm-1am Fri & Sat

L'Estaminet (1, F4)

An eclectic mix of locals drop in to this cosy neigh-bourhood bar, slightly off the tourist track opposite Koningin Astridpark, for equally eclectic (mainly jazz and blues) sounds and good-quality pub food. Weekends are buzziest and the sun terrace is the spot to be in summer.

☎ 050 33 09 16/34 40 52 ✉ Park 5 ☺ 11am-late, closed Mon & Thu

Lokkedize (1, A6)

Locals love this often rowdy, occasionally relaxed, atmospheric backstreet bar with good pub grub and live jazz.

☎ 050 33 38 39 ✉ Korte Vuldersstraat 33 ☺ 5pm-late Thu, Sun & Mon, 3pm-late Fri & Sat

Lumiere Cinema (1, B2)

This much-loved art house cinema offers an excellent programme of foreign films, often in their original language, and is home to the excellent Cinema Novo Film Festival (boxed text, opposite).

☎ 050 34 34 65 ⌨ www.lumiere.be in Dutch & French ✉ St-Jakobsstraat 36

Relax (1, B2)

This hip hop and R&B cocktail bar-cum-dance club is refreshing in a town with too many techno and kara-oke bars. A predominantly black crowd show the rest how it's done to rotating DJs every Friday and Saturday night.

☎ 0474 67 83 55 ✉ St-Jakobsstraat 45 ☺ 8pm-late

De Halve Maan's (p63) beer

Staminee De Garre (1, D3)

This lively local pub, with over 100 beers on offer, is in a 16th-century two-storey house hidden in a narrow lane between the lace shops.

☎ 050 34 10 29 ✉ De Garre 1, off Breidelstraat ☺ noon-midnight Mon-Thu, 11am-1am Fri-Sun

't Brugs Beertje (1, B4)

An offering of around 300 Belgian beers is what attracts most drinkers to this brown pub, but the often off-hand service doesn't keep tourists here for long – locals, how-ever, swear by the place!

☎ 050 33 96 16 ✉ Kemel-straat 5 ☺ 4pm-late Thu-Tue

The Top (1, B5)

The local crowd all know each other at this kooky bar, with colourful mod design, cheap drinks and a DJ spinning unpredictable sounds. The bar is so tiny that before long you'll know everyone too.

☎ 050 33 03 51 ✉ St-Salvatorskerkhof 5 ☺ 8pm-2am

Concertgebouw is Bruges' controversial concert venue

TOP END

Hotel de Orangerie
(1, D4)
This 15th-century convent has been converted into a fantastic 20-room boutique hotel. Its enviable canal-side location (some rooms with views) is superb and the owners have filled the place with antiques and *objets d'art*. If you're with kids, take advantage of the baby-sitting services and head out for a romantic dinner.
☎ 050 34 16 49 ☐ www.hotelorangerie.com ✉ Karthuizerinnenstraat 10 ✗ ♿

Manoir RED! (1, E6)
This early-18th-century building is certainly being put to good use, housing both a hotel and a good restaurant. The eight rooms are spacious, most kitted out in antique style (room 7 is in a modern Italian style) and there's a lovely terrace, an atmospheric bar and salon and a great garden that's used during summer.
☎ 050 33 70 70 ☐ www.manoirred.com ✉ Nieuwe Gentweg 53 ✗ ♿

Relais Ravestein (1, F2)
For those who crave 'design hotel' style no matter what city they're in, the Ravestein is your Bruges address. The 15 suites housed in a fine canal-side location come in several shapes and sizes and all have Jacuzzi, flat-screen TV and free wi-fi. There's a decent hotel restaurant and several excellent ones nearby on Langestraat.
☎ 050 47 69 47 ☐ www.relaisravestein.be ✉ Molenmeers 11 ✗ ♿ ♿

WEEKEND SPECIALS?
While Brussels empties out on weekends, Bruges fills to overflowing with visitors from France and the UK looking for a romantic getaway, an art-filled sojourn or just an excuse to drink plenty of marvellous beers. So if you must visit on weekends, book well ahead and prepare to pay a premium over mid-week rates.

Romantik Pandhotel
(1, E4)
Tucked away on a pretty tree-lined street just a few minutes' walk from the Markt, this is an intimate, attractive, richly decorated hotel. A former carriage house, all 23 rooms are individually decorated with fascinating *objets d'art*, but has all the mod-cons you could wish for. The service is warm, the breakfast eggs hot and the ambiance romantic.
☎ 050 34 06 66 ☐ www.pandhotel.com ✉ Pandreitje 16 ✗

MIDRANGE

Anselmus Hotel (1, E2)
This lovely little hotel doesn't get much attention, but it's one of our Bruges favourites. Housed in a handsome 16th-century mansion, the rooms are spacious, scrupulously clean and decorated in a suitably antique style. The breakfasts are satisfying, the staff welcoming and it's a very quiet hotel at night, making it a great little romantic hideaway.
☎ 050 34 13 74 ☐ www.anselmus.be ✉ Riddersstraat 15 ✗

Boating past Hotel de Orangerie

Good times at Bauhaus' popular bar

Hotel Adornes
Situated on a quiet stretch of the St-Annarei canal, this hidden gem of a hotel offers 20 rooms decorated in a tasteful and understated manner. The buffet breakfast is taken in an attractive room with an open fire and there's a small bar for those cold nights in. It's a child-friendly address, with cots available, and the hotel offers complimentary pushbikes and parking.
☎ 050 34 13 36 ☐ www.adornes.be ✉ St-Annarei 26

Montanus Hotel (1, E6)
While not centrally located, this stylish hotel's position just adds to the sense of tranquillity. Of the 24 rooms, some are located in the garden wing (on the other side of a massive garden), while in the main building, facing the road, are the spacious suites. The public spaces are quite chic and the staff are very accommodating.
☎ 050 33 11 76 ☐ www.montanus.be

✉ Nieuwe Gentweg 78

BUDGET

Bauhaus
With everything from dorms to doubles, this hostel/hotel is a popular hangout for young travellers who hang out in its café-bar. It's friendly and clean, they provide sheets and towels and if you want private showers book the hotel section which is now rated as one-star digs.
☎ 050 34 10 93 ☐ www.bauhaus.be ✉ Langestraat 135

Hotel Ter Reien (1, F2)
This is a decent, clean hotel in a great location with rooms that offer fantastic canal views that are almost Venetian. The staff are friendly and the breakfast is filling. They have triple and quadruple rooms – as well as a charming honeymoon suite.
☎ 050 34 91 00 ☐ www.hotelterreien.be ✉ Langestraat 1

Hotel Van Eyck (1, B4)
This converted mansion, dating back to the 18th-century, has eight rooms (in varying states of renovation) accessed by a head-spinning spiral staircase, with the larger rooms being worth the extra cash. The simple breakfast is taken in a lovely breakfast room – with a relaxing soundtrack – and the hotel has wi-fi. The two guys that run it are very friendly.
☎ 050 33 52 67 ☐ www.hotelvaneyck.be ✉ Korte Zilverstraat 7

Passage (1, A5)
While we just love the atmosphere of the restaurant and bar (p68) here, the shared rooms (upstairs) have left us a little cold, unfortunately. However, the hotel (next door) offers good, clean rooms (all renovated in 2004) that are great value and the staff here are accommodating and friendly. Excellent value.
☎ 050 34 02 32 ☐ www.passagebruges.com ✉ Dweersstraat 26-28

Bruges was founded around the ninth century, but like many other Flemish cities, the textile industry is what really put it on the map. Much of this trade was with England and by the 13th century, Bruges was a major player in the textile trade. However with the increased wealth came increased taxes and Bruges' guildsmen refused to pay up when a new round were introduced in 1302. The subsequent revolt (known as Bruges Matins or Bruges Metten) saw the defeat of the French garrison and six weeks later the defeat of the French near Kortrijk in the Battle of the Golden Spurs. While the French regained control, the defeat is still celebrated on 11 July.

> **UNESCO**
> Bruges' medieval charm is official, having been placed on the World Heritage List in 2000 for its Gothic architecture and as the birthplace of important Flemish Primitive artists such as Jan Van Eyck and Hans Memling.

Despite more unrest, Bruges remained a powerful city in the wool trade and prosperity continued under the rule of the dukes of Burgundy in the late 1400s. Flemish art flourished during the 1400s, with artists such as Jan Van Eyck producing works with luminous colours and intricate detail. While the artistic flow was strong, the Zwin, the waterway connecting Bruges to the sea, silted up and efforts to create another sea link were unsuccessful. The city's role as part of the Hanseatic League (a group of powerful northern European trading cities) lessened, with the headquarters moving to Antwerp. A former giant of industry in Europe quickly became a sleeping one for over 400 years.

The revival of Bruges only began in the late 1800s and attention was drawn to it by the publication of *Bruges-la-Morte* (Bruges the Dead), Georges Rodenbach's acclaimed 1892 novel in which Bruges is used as a metaphor for the protagonist's dead wife. In 1907 a new canal linked Bruges to the new port of Zeebrugge and while Zeebrugge was badly damaged in both world wars, Bruges miraculously escaped unharmed.

Today, Bruges is the capital of West-Vlaanderen and its income is derived mainly from tourism.

A devout statue outside Onze-Lieve-Vrouwekerk (p64)

Belgium's second-biggest city is by far its hippest. Antwerp (Antwerpen in Flemish, Anvers in French) has always been a hotbed of creativity, from the works of revered local Pieter Paul Rubens in the 1600s to the startling fashion entrance of the Antwerp 6 in the 1990s. Rubens' art hangs in several sites around the city and the work of the Antwerp 6 (as well as several new designers coming on strong) are found hanging in boutiques that resemble contemporary art galleries.

Part of a Rubens triptych in the Onze Lieve Vrouwekathedraal (p78)

The prodigious output of these designers has made Antwerp the nation's fashion capital and a fantastic place to shop. Besides the clothing boutiques, there are antiques, diamond stores and chocolate shops with window displays that are as artful as they are enticing. Once you tire of that, you'll need a disco nap as the nightlife in Antwerp is the best in the country, with summer parties starting in the sunshine and ending as the sun rises again. In winter it just moves indoors. If you prefer to sip a beer in genial surrounds and try some *jenever* (local gin), bar-hopping a couple of blocks can take all night. Dining is also super in Antwerp, everything from fantastic fries to truly great plates at restaurants such as Gin Fish.

The historic centre is also snow-dome cute. The impressive cathedral can take you a couple of hours to visit and the pretty Grote Markt on which it stands is an inspiring sight.

A Rubens statue with Onze Lieve Vrouwkathedraal (p78) in the background

Belgium's fashion capital is a fabulous small city that's as beautiful as Bruges and Ghent, is more authentic in many ways, is immensely walkable, and has many fascinating neighbourhoods that are a joy to explore.

It's stylish **heart** is centred around the glorious Grote Markt – arguably the finest of any Belgian city with its many gorgeous gabled guildhouses and Brabo fountain at its centre – with jazz clubs, karaoke bars, mussels restaurants and smoky cafés keeping it real. Adjoining this is the smaller Handschoenmarkt, more touristy but fronting on to the stunning Onze Lieve Vrouwekathedraal.

In the area immediately south of the Grote Markt you'll find cobblestone streets lined with awesome restaurants, such as Gin Fish, atmospheric bars like De Vagant, beautiful B&Bs and great shops. A couple of kilometres south of the wonderful Vrijdagmarkt square are Oever and Kloosterstraat, a long atmospheric street lined with antique and bric-a-brac shops, and 20th-century design stores. Parallel to this is Nationalestraat, Antwerp's most stylish street lined with the best of Belgian designers and home to many flagship stores of the Antwerp 6. Off Nationalestraat is Kammenstraat, a funky street lined with skate shops and alternative fashion. These streets all lead to the Zuid (South) area, home to Antwerp's best museums and art galleries, wonderful Art Nouveau architecture, atmospheric cafés, excellent restaurants, buzzy bars and groovy dance clubs. This is the area to head to on a Friday or Saturday night or just as equally on the weekend when locals bask in the sun outside cafés.

East of the Grote Markt is the Groenplaats and the commercial centre, and the Meir, the main pedestrian street, where you'll find global franchises and the Inno department store. South of here, heading in the direction of the station, you'll find (in this order) exclusive designer stores, the theatre area, the daily market, the diamond district and the station.

North of the station is **Chinatown** and to the north and northeast of that a slightly seedy area leading to the **red-light district** and beyond that the port area. This area is being developed and along Brouwersvliet and Oudeleeuwenrui, and the surrounding streets, you'll find a smattering of great restaurants, bars, and clubs.

To the west of all of this is the Scheldt river, which you can see from the water on a cruise or with a drink in hand from the Zuiderterras.

Just another wonderful antique shop

RUBENS

Pieter Paul Rubens (1577–1640) was one of many Flemish artists who studied and worked in Italy, returning to produce work of staggering scale, vibrancy and use of colour. Many of his works can be seen around Antwerp, at the Onze Lieve Vrouwekathedraal (p78), Koninklijk Museum voor Schone Kunsten (left), Rockoxhuis (p78), St-Jackobskerk (8, D2), Rubenshuis (p78) as well as Brussels' Musées Royaux des Beaux-Arts de Belgique (p15).

FotoMuseum
This brilliant museum of photography holds alternating exhibitions of its enormous collection, around themes such as Landscape, Body and Identity, and adventurous temporary shows by international photographers. There's an excellent bookshop.
03 242 93 00 Waalse Kaai 10am-6pm Tue-Sun €6/free/4

Grote Markt (8, B2)
This square, lined with guildhalls, is watched over by the Stadhuis (town hall). Its Brabo Fountain explains the fable of Antwerp's naming: Roman warrior Silvius Brabo killed a giant, Druon Antigon, who had a habit of chopping off the hands of shipmasters who refused to pay river toll. Brabo chopped off the giant's hand, tossed it into the river (*hand werpen* means hand throwing) and Antwerpen grew.

Koninklijk Museum voor Schone Kunsten
Flanders' largest art collection – over 7000 pieces – is housed at the excellent Royal Museum of Fine Arts, including masterpieces by Peter Paul Rubens, Jan Van Eyck, Hans Memling, Jacob Jordaens and René Magritte.
03 238 78 09 Plaatsnijdersstraat 2 10am-5pm Tue-Sun €6/free/4

TERRY CARTER
Rockoxhuis (p78)

Mode Museum (MoMu) (8, B3)
This excellent Fashion Museum has two five-month-long exhibitions a year, generally curated in conjunction with designers, to explore, through themes, the social and cultural context of their inspiration and work.
03 470 27 70 Nationalestraat 28 10am-8pm Tue-Sun, call ahead as it's closed between exhibits €7/free/5

MuHKA (8, A4)
Recent exhibitions at this exciting Museum of Contemporary Art have included a survey of contemporary conceptual art from Vancouver as part of an initiative where the museum invites artists to exhibit work in direct dialogue with art from the museum's collection and curate an accompanying exhibition of other artists' work.
03 260 99 99 Leuvenstraat 32 10am-5pm Tue-Sun €6/free/4

Museum Mayer Van den Bergh (8, C4)
This wonderful 1904 townhouse in a 16th-century style was established by art collector Fritz Mayer Van den Bergh's mother after his death, to house his extraordinary collection of treasures: over 3000 works of Western art, paintings, sculptures, decorative arts, tapestries, carpets and stained glass.
03 232 42 37
Lange Gasthuisstraat 19
10am-5pm Tue-Sun
€4/free/3, combined ticket incl Rubenshuis €6

Museum Plantin-Moretus (8, B3)
The city's finest museum in the former grand home of a prosperous 16th- and 17th-

TERRY CARTER
Volkskundemuseum (p78)

Outside Nationaal
Scheepvaartmuseum

century printing family tells us
as much about how they lived,
through its exquisite architecture, interiors and decorative
arts, as it does about early
printing. A rare copy of the
Gutenberg Bible is on display.
☎ 03 221 14 50
✉ Vrijdagmarkt 22
☼ 10am-5pm Tue-Sun
€ €6/free/4

Nationaal Scheepvaart-museum (8, A2)
This maritime museum,
occupying an imposing 13th-century fortification right on
the Scheldt river, displays
nautical instruments,
intricate models of ships,
paintings and other maritime
paraphernalia.
☎ 03 201 93 40
✉ Steenplein 1
☼ 10am-5pm Tue-Sun
€ €4/free/3

Onze Lieve Vrouwekathedraal (8, B2)
As much art museum as
church, Belgium's largest
Gothic cathedral, ravaged by
fires over the years, remarkably contains some magnificent triptychs by Rubens.
The free guided tours are
fascinating.
☎ 03 213 99 40
✉ Handschoenmarkt
☼ 10am-5pm Mon-Fri,
10am-3pm Sat & 1-4pm Sun
€ €2/free/1.50

Rockoxhuis (8, C2)
Like the Museum Plantin-Moretus, this former residence
of Antwerp's burgomaster
(mayor), Nicolaas Rockox
(1560-1640), now a museum
of 17th-century art, gives a
great insight into how a noble
family lived during that period.
☎ 03 231 47 10 ✉ Keizer-straat 12 ☼ 10am-5pm
Tue-Sun € €6/free/4

Rubenshuis (8, D3)
The city's top tourist spot,
Rubenshuis as a museum
is somewhat disappointing
after Rockoxhuis and Plantin
Moretus, giving little insight
into how Rubens lived. There
are some impressive paintings here, however — save
some time to appreciate *The
Annunciation*.
☎ 03 201 15 55 ✉ Wapper
9-11 ☼ 10am-5pm Tue-Sun
€ €5/free/2.50, combined
ticket incl Museum Mayer
Van den Bergh €6

Etnografisch Museum

St-Carolus-Borromeuskerk (8, C2)
Rubens was responsible for
much of the decoration of this
ornate Jesuit baroque church,
built from 1615–21. Although
39 ceiling paintings created by
his studio were destroyed in a
fire in 1718, it's still splendid
and worth a look.
☎ 03 231 3751 ✉ Hendrik
Conscienceplein ☼ 10am-
12.30pm & 2-5pm Mon-Sat
€ free

Volkskundemuseum (8, B2)
This charming Folklore
Museum, the oldest in the
country, explores everyday
life in Antwerp through
thousands of intriguing
objects organised in collections based on subjects such
as festivals, rituals, death
and so on. If you enjoy this,
check out the engaging
Etnografisch Museum
(☎ 03 220 86 00; Suikerrui
19) around the corner.
☎ 03 220 86 66 ✉ Gilde-kamersstraat 2-6 ☼ 10am-
5pm Tue-Sun € €3/free/2,
combined ticket incl Etno-grafisch Museum €4

SIGHT SAVINGS
Look out for reduced combination tickets that allow you
to get into two or three museums and keep in mind
that most museums are free on the last Wednesday of
the month.

BELGIAN DESIGNERS

Ann Demeulemeester

Take time to browse in the big airy flagship store of one of the original Antwerp 6 (p80). Ann Demeulemeester's style exudes an edgy Gothic elegance – her collections are often dominated by black (or slate, grey, or white), are always sleek, sexy and strong, and never lacking attitude.
☎ 03 216 01 33 ✉ Verlatstraat 38 ⊙ 10am-6pm Mon-Sat

Shop till you drop in Antwerp

Christa Reniers (8, B3)

Belgium's best-loved jewellery designer is known best for her hands-on approach, creating many of her products herself, if not closely supervising production from her Brussels atelier. Working in sterling silver mostly, her finely sculpted jewellery and decorative objects have a very organic form, often embellished with exquisite gems and stones.
☎ 03 233 26 02 ✉ Vrijdagmarkt 8 ⊙ noon-6pm Tue-Thu, 10am-1pm & 2-6.30pm Fri & Sat

Coccodrillo (8, C4)

Well-heeled locals head to this elegant store, in the business for over 20 years and one of the few to stock soles by all of Antwerp's top designers – Ann Demeulemeester, Veronique Branquinho, Dries Van Noten, Dirk Bikkembergs, Martin Margiela and AF Vandevorst – in addition to big European names such as Miu Miu, Prada and Chloe.
☎ 03 233 20 93 ✉ Schuttershofstraat 9 ⊙ 10am-6pm Mon-Sat

Garde-robe nationale (8, B4)

Once the striking, vibrant window display (Guatemala-inspired when we last passed by) entices you inside, you'll find collections by Victor Victoria, Pierre Gaspari, Just in Case by Vicky Vinck and Katrien Strijbol.
☎ 03 485 86 87 ✉ Nationalestraat 72 ⊙ 10am-6pm Mon-Sat

Het Modepaleis (8, B3)

Antwerp 6 designer Dries Van Noten's gorgeous flagship store (worth visiting for the architecture alone) stocks

SHOPPING STREETS

- Nationalestraat & side streets (8, B3) – Antwerp 6 and other adventurous Antwerp/Belgian designers
- Kammenstraat (8, B3) – independent designers, retro, vintage and second-hand clothes, streetwear and skate/snowboard gear – the place to get your dreadies, piercings and tattoos
- Huidevettersstraat, Komedieplaats & Schuttershofstraat (8, C3) – exclusive designer brands such as Cartier, Gucci, Louis Vuitton, Ralph Lauren and Longchamps
- Kloosterstraat (8, A4) – antiques, *brocante* (bric-a-brac), retro furniture, decorative and design objects
- Lange Koepoortstraat & Wolstaat (8, B2 & C2) – wonderful little art galleries, bookshops, second-hand CDs and specialist music stores
- Leysstraat & Meir (8, D3) – high street stores like H&M, Mango, Zara, Morgan, Replay, Diesel, Energie, Footlocker, Body Shop and Inno department store

his splendid collections of wearable men's clothes. Guys can conservatively stick with superbly tailored shirts, trousers and suits, or daringly add a wild printed shirt, flamboyant flowing scarf or matador-style jacket!
☎ 03 470 25 10 ⊠ Nationalestraat 16 🕑 10am-6pm Mon-Sat

Louis (8, B3)
A one-stop-shop for the Antwerp 6 designers and other local stars, Raf Simons, Haider Ackermann and Veronique Leroy, along with interesting international designers such as Rick Owens.
☎ 02 280 26 66 ⊠ Lombardenvest 2 🕑 10am-6pm Mon-Sat

Veronique Branquinho
A very eclectic designer, the common elements among Branquinho's collections are her use of black, silver and grey, beguiling bold prints, and an androgynous style. A recent range featured moody prints of moonlit lakes and floaty black chiffon capes, while her more casual

looks are often flatteringly layered.
☎ 03 233 66 16 ⊠ Nationalestraat 73 🕑 10.30am-6.30pm Mon-Sat

Verso (8, C4)
This sleek black designer department store stocks swish labels such as Prada, Alexander McQueen, D&G, Costume National and Paul Smith, and Belgian designers Dirk Bikkembergs, Kris Van Assche and Dirk Schonberger, along with cosmetics from Stephane Marais, By Terry, Aesop and Skin Ethics. There's a very cool café-bar.
☎ 03 226 92 92 ⊠ Lange Gasthuisstraat 11 🕑 10am-6pm Mon-Sat

Walter (8, B4)
Walter Van Beirendonck's audacious fashion – characterised by a whacky combination of vibrant colours, cheeky graphics, bold prints, intriguing details and ironic messages – is inspired by hybrid cultures and global politics, and is provocative and wearable stuff. A visit to his warehouse-style store-cum-gallery is a must.

☎ 03 213 26 44 ⊠ St-Antoniusstraat 12 🕑 10am-6pm Mon-Sat

CLOTHING & ACCESSORIES

De Groene Wolk (8, C3)
Antwerp's best children's clothes store stocks fabulous European labels, including Antwerp designers – Anne Kurris, Max & Lola, Nineteenfifty, Belle Rose and Juicy Courture – and encourages parents to dress their kids more imaginatively, with window displays that might team khaki jackets with frothy ballerina tutus, or Hawaiian shirts with tweed.
☎ 03 234 18 47 ⊠ Korte Gasthuisstraat 20 🕑 noon-3pm & 7-11pm Mon-Fri

Fish & Chips (8, B3)
At this urban street gear supermarket you'll find a DJ playing, break-dancing events, a lounge with playstations, a dog sliding down a slippery dip to a chill-out tunnel downstairs (we don't kid), graffiti spray paints, comic books, action figures,

THE LEGEND OF THE ANTWERP 6
Renowned for putting Antwerp on the fashion map, and with their idiosyncratic collections and seasonal shows now eagerly awaited, the Antwerp 6 – Ann Demeulemeester, Dries Van Noten, Dirk Van Saene, Dirk Bikkembergs, Marina Yee and Walter Van Beirendonck – are infamous for their audacious start in the business. Still fairly fresh graduates from the Koninklijke Academie voor Schone Kunsten, Antwerp's fashion school, in 1986 they loaded their collections onto a truck, and took off to London where they showed their provocative stuff among bridal wear at a fashion show! Having attracted sufficient attention, they went their separate ways, each establishing a reputation for producing distinctive designs with attitude, and maintaining bases in Antwerp, helping Flanders develop its fashion reputation. The Academie continues to churn out cutting-edge designers – look out for Martin Margiela, AF Vandevorst, Veronique Branquinho, Bernhard Willhelm, Jurgi Peersons and Raf Simons.

TERRY CARTER

Lucky Brand Jeans

skateboard gear, brands like Religion, Meltin Pot, Box Fresh and Kana Beach, Goorin hats, and Killah, Etnics, Vans and És sneakers.
☎ 03 227 08 24 ✉ Kammenstraat 36-38 ⌚ 10am-6.30pm Mon-Sat

Hit (8, B3)
This cool store is one of a few to stock more funky casual gear by Antwerp designers, such as local brand G-Star, along with Nolita de Nimes, Cute Combo tees, and an enormous range of Freitag bags.
☎ 02 226 02 31 ✉ Kammenstraat 42 ⌚ 10am-6pm Mon-Sat

Huis A Boon (8, B3)
This charming old-fashioned store, founded in 1884, has over 10,000 types of fine leather gloves in antique wooden drawers. The owner takes her craft seriously, hand-fitting the gloves to make sure you leave with the perfect size, and ensuring her range of colours are in keeping with latest fashions.
☎ 03 232 23 87 ✉ Lombardenvest 2-4 ⌚ 11am-6pm Mon-Sat

Lucky Brand Jeans (8, B3)
The first European store of this popular American brand specialises in comfy jeans in a range of cuts and bo-ho gear – pretty retro-print skirts, embroidered khaki jackets, Hawaiian print shirts and Bob Dylan tees. Don't leave without checking out the ceiling – your parents' record collection by any chance?
☎ 03 227 10 48 ✉ Kammenstraat 43 ⌚ 10am-6pm Mon-Sat

Sussies (8, B3)
This is *the* place to come for cool retro clothes, shoes, accessories and furniture – everything from colourful ponchos to 1980s hot pink pointy-toed knee-high boots, to star-shaped wall clocks and Panton chairs.
☎ 03 280 26 66 ✉ Oude Koornmarkt 69 ⌚ 1-6pm Mon, Tue-Sat 11am-6pm

Zappa (8, B4)
This vibrant little store is home to the funkiest shoes, boots and sneakers from Fly, Chie Mihara, Camper, Jocomomola, Aeffe and

Tsubo, and the shoe of the moment, the Ras black furry boots with pom poms!
☎ 03 293 85 07 ✉ Kammenstraat 74 ⌚ 10am-6pm Mon-Sat

ANTIQUES & DESIGN

Cru (8, A4)
If you simply must take something home after ogling all the funky furniture and design objects on Kloosterstraat, then head here to pick up a vintage Murano vase or cool chrome clock from the sixties.
☎ 03 231 88 86 ✉ St-Michielstraat 19 ⌚ 1-6pm Wed-Sun

Design Gallery (8, A4)
Fancy some groovy seats from the Pompidou perhaps? What makes this collection of rare 20th-century Belgian and European furniture so special is that owner Michael Marcy has been collecting for 30 years and has an eye for the unusual, so you won't see similar pieces elsewhere.
☎ 03 248 98 00

TERRY CARTER
Cru sells 20th-century collectables

✉ Arsenaalstraat 5
🕑 2-6pm Wed-Sun

Flowermountain (8, F2)
You won't have difficulty picking up an Arne Jacobsen or Eames chair here, with Antwerp's largest and funkiest collection of 20th-century design stretching across the ground floor and basement of Antwerp's Design Centre.
☎ 0475 690 787 ✉ Lange Winkelhaakstraat 26
🕑 11am-6pm Mon-Sat

Full Effect (8, A4)
While the collection of groovy 20th-century furniture (with an emphasis on the '50s and '60s) is small, the quality is high: their showpiece is the much-coveted 1968 Swedish Torlan 'Ovalia' egg-shaped chair – price on application!
☎ 0485 273 282 ✉ Kloosterstraat 44a 🕑 1-6pm Fri-Wed

BOOKS & MUSIC

Chelsea (8, A3)
If you went to Lucky Brand (p81) and saw your parents' record collection on the ceiling, then head here to see it again, along with your grandparents', and your own treasured vinyls from childhood. Specialising in second-hand LPs, singles, 78s, EPs and CDs of all genres, you're bound to find something special to take you back in time.
☎ 03 233 85 77
✉ Kloosterstraat 10
🕑 11am-6pm Tue-Sat, 1-5pm Sun & holidays

Copyright (8, B3)
Specialising in gorgeous, glossy arts, architecture, design and fashion books, it's appropriate that this stylish store is located on the ground floor of MoMu (p77). Along with fine coffee-table

books and cutting-edge texts, you'll find super exhibition catalogues produced by MoMu.
☎ 03 232 94 16
✉ Nationalestraat 28A
🕑 11am-6.30pm Tue-Sat & 2-5.30pm Sun

FOOD

Goossens (8, C3)
Definitely the best bakery in the city since 1884, and perhaps one of the best in the world – you'll smell it before you see it! Locals line up for their olive bread, raisin loafs and *suikerbrood* (sweet bread).
☎ 03 226 07 91 ✉ Korte Gasthuisstraat 31 🕑 8am-7pm Tue-Sat

Philip's Biscuits (8, C3)
You'll find every kind of biscuit imaginable from the popular butter biscuits to macaroons and biscuits flavoured with spices, from ginger to cinnamon, but we don't care what's inside, we just love the retro tins!
☎ 03 231 26 60 ✉ Korte Gasthuisstraat 11 🕑 10am-6pm Mon-Sat

Pierre Marcolini (8, C3)
This award-winning chocolate maker specialises in fine chocolates in elegant packaging, along with wonderful chocolate pastries. Their heavenly Envol and Aurore sweets have won prizes in the World Patisserie Championships – look at them and you'll know why, taste them and you'll be heading right back for more.
☎ 03 226 50 01 ✉ Huidevettersstraat 38-40
🕑 10am-6pm Mon-Sat

TERRY CARTER

Mouth-watering goodies at Goossens

Bar Italia

Italian €€

This three-storey Italian joint has been wildly popular for as long as we can remember – when you're still turning away customers without bookings on weekends for this long, you must be doing something right. And what they do right is serving up very decent pizzas and pastas along with friendly service and a no-nonsense wine list.

☎ 03 216 17 48 ✉ Graaf Van Egmontstraat 59 ☽ noon-2.30pm & 6.30-11pm Mon-Fri, 5-11pm Sat & Sun Ⓥ

Brasserie Den Artist

Belgian brasserie €€

Busy from the first coffee to the last beer, this charming brasserie has a great ambiance. Even better are the hearty Belgian dishes (the steaks are a favourite) and great soups served up to a regular clientele. Make sure to check out the backboard menu for specials.

☎ 03 238 09 95 ✉ Museumstraat 45 ☽ 8.30am-1am

Brasserie National (8, B3)

Contemporary Italian €€€

This gorgeous dining room in the ModeNatie – the building that also houses

Brasserie Den Artist

MoMu (p77) and a fashion school – is just the place for a postmuseum visit. Those wanting to stay skinny as a supermodel can stick to the wonderful fresh salads, others will find it hard to resist dishes such as the risotto with *merguez* (spicy Moroccan sausages). Great selection of wines by the glass.

☎ 03 227 56 56 ✉ Nationalestraat 32 ☽ 11am-9.30pm Tue-Sun

Chilli Club

Asian €€

This casual Asian eatery packs in locals who come for the great 'tapas' and wok-tossed specials – the noodles are excellent and the open kitchen full of action.

☎ 03 248 90 90 ✉ De Burburestraat 43 ☽ 7-11pm Ⓥ

De Kleine Zavel (8, A3)

French/Flemish €€€

While this restaurant comes highly recommended, it appears to be coasting a little on its reputation. The menu is an excellent read, however when we visited the cooking was merely competent

'FRENCH' FRIES

Call them what you will, Belgian fries are the best in the world. While the French claim to have invented them, there are several explanations as to why they're called French fries. But what's in a name? It's what's in the fries that counts. Firstly, Belgian fries are made from Bintje potatoes, the best coming from Belgium or the Netherlands. Secondly, they must be cut about 1cm squared – any smaller and they absorb too much oil and can burn easily. Thirdly, they're twice cooked; first at a lower temperature and then, after resting, at a higher temperature to get that crisp on the outside, soft on the inside when you bite into one. There's a bewildering array of sauces available – but mayonnaise is a great place to start! After much research, we've decided that our favourite *frittur* is here in Antwerp. At the **vogeltjesmarkt** (8, D4; Theaterplein; ☽ Sat & Sun), look for the caravan called **Jabbe Dabbe Doe**. These women know their fries.

and the chipped plates and dirty-smocked chefs didn't inspire confidence. Still, it's an atmospheric space and locals swear it's one of the best in town.
☎ 03 231 96 91 ✉ Stoofstraat 2 ☯ noon-2pm Sun-Fri, 6-10.30pm Sun-Thu, 6.30-11pm Fri & Sat

Dock's Café (8, B1)
French/Italian/seafood €€€
A mainstay on the Antwerp dining scene, Dock's is the kind of place your boss takes you to in Antwerp. The food served in the large split-level space is quality stuff, but we prefer the oyster bar with its always fresh oysters.
☎ 03 226 63 30 ✉ Jordaenskaai 7 ☯ noon-2.30pm Mon-Fri, 6-11pm

Mon-Thu, 6pm-midnight Fri-Sat, noon-10.30pm Sun

Frittur No 1 (8, B3)
Belgian fries €
Almost an obligatory stop when visiting the Grote Markt area, the golden fries served up here are a delight. perfect for soaking up the alcohol after a few too many of those potent beers. What makes Belgian fries so good? See the boxed text on p83.
✉ Hoogstraat 1 ☯ 24hr

Gin Fish (8, B2)
Contemporary Seafood €€€€
Chef Didier Garnich (box, below) shocked Antwerp by transforming his Michelin-starred De Matelote restaurant into a 13-seat place

where all diners sit at a bar in front of an open kitchen. However, Didier's on to something special here. He's relaxed and comfortable performing in front of a salivating audience, working with the freshest ingredients imaginable, and no printed menu. He simply dishes up whatever he thinks works best for the produce available. Book well ahead.
☎ 03 231 32 07 ✉ Haarstraat 9 ☯ 6-10pm Tue-Sat

Grand Café Horta (8, D4)
Café/brasserie €€
A great stop after taking in Rubenshuis (p78), this is a very grand café indeed. You can nibble on anything from

TERRY CARTER

DIDIER GARNICH
Chef Didier Garnich won himself a Michelin star for his refined seafood cooking at his Matelote restaurant. And while foodies were dismayed when he decided to hand back the accolade, his replacement restaurant has perhaps made more waves than he expected. Working to a captive audience of 13 who sit at a long bar around his stainless steel kitchen, he now cooks without a menu, but with a head full of recipes that get called up when the right ingredients arrive on his doorstep – every day.

Wannabe celebrity chefs will find it both exciting and disheartening to see a chef of this calibre up close. The kitchen is immaculate all night, the atmosphere focused but calm, and the chef relaxed enough to explain every dish in several languages to his rapt audience. This is not the stuff of a drama-filled reality cooking show, but Michelin thought Didier's performances were good enough to make him a star – Gin Fish (above) received its first in 2006.

Too-kool-for-skool Gusto

ciabatta to mussels while taking in the airy glass-and-girders setting.

☎ 03 232 28 15
✉ Hopland 2 ⏰ 9am-11pm Sun-Thu, 9am-midnight Fri & Sat, kitchen from 11am daily **V**

Gusto (8, B3)
Contemporary Mediterranean €€€
This is a hip space that manages to be übercool but still friendly enough to make you want to drop in to for a drink. Chef-owner Patrick serves up great antipasti, pastas and interesting main courses, with delicious bread and olive oil to dip into while you check out the décor. There's a short, well-chosen wine list.

☎ 03 239 23 90
✉ Steenhouwersvest 29
⏰ 11am-10.30pm Tue-Sun

Het Pomphuis
Brasserie €€€
While this is a bit out of the city centre, it's well worth the trek for both the phenomenal old pump-house setting and the refined brasserie fare. Despite the atmospheric (and dramatic) setting of the interior, the

outdoor tables are prime positions when the weather is agreeable.

☎ 03 770 86 25
✉ Siberiastraat 7
⏰ 10am-midnight, kitchen noon-2.30 & 6-10.30pm

Lucy Chang
Chinese/Asian €€
This endearingly cute and fun 'oriental market' style restaurant still packs them in even after a few years of trading its tasty pan-Asian cuisine. There's a variety of seating (outdoors in summer as well) and the food is inexpensive enough for you to order a few dishes and work your way through them in classic Asian style. No bookings and no credit cards.

☎ 03 248 95 60
✉ Marnixplaats 16-17
⏰ noon-midnight **V**

O tagine
Moroccan €€€
With a sizeable Moroccan community in Antwerp it was only a matter of time that the miracle of Moroccan cooking, the tagine, had a place to shine. While the décor would be considered over-the-top in Marrakech,

the tagines presented here would be right at home. There's also a hookah lounge.

☎ 03 237 06 19 ✉ Leopold de Waelstraat 20 ⏰ 10am-midnight Tue-Sun **V**

Pazzo
Mediterranean/Japanese €€
With its odd menu mixing Italian and Japanese ingredients, Pazzo could be dreadful. Thankfully the menu's mix of tempura and tapenade doesn't taste as strange as it sounds and even attracts the lunch-time work crowd who are generally more interested in getting a few drinks in than what's on the plates. The bar upstairs has an extensive number of great wines by the glass.

☎ 03 232 86 82 ✉ Oude Leeuwenrui 12 ⏰ noon-3pm & 6-11pm Mon-Fri, bar from 3pm

Renzo (8, B3)
Italian snacks €
This great little shopping-district eatery is perfect for those who just want to refuel quickly before working on maxing out their credit cards. The panini and

ciabattas are all tasty and the coffee is Italian-style – the perfect pick-me-up before hitting the streets again.
☎ 03 225 06 10
✉ Kammenstraat 30
☼ 10am-7pm Mon-Sat ♿

Rimbaud (8, D1)
Seafood €€€
This alluring little 20-seat restaurant is the work of chef Dave de Croebele who, offering a simple fixed three-course menu, is relaxed enough to personally explain it to every table, and

talented enough to head back into the kitchen and produce some truly mouth-watering meals. Dave worked with Didier Garnich (see boxed text, p84) and has the same approach to cooking fish, making this one of Antwerp's best seafood eateries.
☎ 03 226 79 70 ✉ Hessenbrug 5 ☼ noon-1.30pm & 7-9.30pm Mon-Fri

Rooden Hoed (8, B2)
Belgian/French €€€
Despite this elegant restaurant being almost within

arms reach of the cathedral, it manages to avoid being a tourist-driven affair. While the mussels are the specialty of the house (and the fries are not bad either), they do beautifully cooked beef and pork for those not fond of bivalve molluscs. Great fixed-price menus and respectable wines by the glass. Divine desserts.
☎ 03 233 28 44 ✉ Oude Koornmarkt 25 ☼ noon-2.30pm & 6-10.30pm Mon-Thu, 6-11pm Fri-Sat, 6-10pm Sun

Soep & Soup (8, B4)
Soup €
During the colder months this popular fashion-district place gets packed with people warming up with one of the five soups on the blackboard menu every day. The minestrone is a meal in itself.
☎ 03 707 28 05
✉ Kammenstraat 89
☼ Mon-Sat 11am-7pm
♿ Ⓥ

Sombat Thai Cuisine (8, B1)
Thai €€
This graceful Thai restaurant is *the* one that Antwerp locals agree is the best in town. With its stylish paper-umbrella-adorned ceiling and attentive service, they're probably right. However, Thai aficionados will find most flavours here a little too soft for their taste so ask them to turn up the heat a little – they'll happily oblige.
☎ 03 226 21 90
✉ Vleeshuisstraat 1
☼ noon-2.30pm Tue-Fri, 6-11pm Tue-Sun

Petite Rimbaud: one of Antwerp's best new eateries

CAFÉS

Berlin (8, B4)
One of those buzzy cafés that hum with the chatter of friends and family enjoying a coffee or casual bite together, it's ideally located for a caffeine fix mid-shopping.
☎ 03 227 11 01
✉ Kleine Markt 1-3
🕑 7.30am-late Mon-Fri, 10am-late Sat & Sun

Canal
This low-key Zuid café is popular with locals who pop in to read the paper and have a drink or a delicious ciabatta. Cosy in winter, its sun terrace is one of the hottest spots in summer.
☎ 03 237 27 00
✉ Leopold de Waelplaats 2
🕑 8am-late Mon-Fri, 10am-late Sat & Sun

Hangar 41
This big, breezy, bright space on the waterfront is beautifully designed – a wonderful place for a coffee or drink any time of the day or night. The food is tasty too!
☎ 03 257 09 18
✉ St-Michielskaai 41

LOCAL EVENTS
Jazz Middelheim (www.jazzmiddelheim.be) – A biennial, week-long jazz festival held in the second week of August

🕑 9am-late Mon-Fri, 10am-late Sun & Sun

Ultimatum (8, B2)
The best spot for a casual drink on the Grote Markt, for its sublime views (especially at night with the town hall and guildhouses lit up), good Belgian beers and decent wines by the glass.
☎ 03 232 58 53 ✉ Grote Markt 8 🕑 11am-11pm

BARS & PUBS

Bar*Dak
It's hard to believe that this tiny candlelit black bar (with its funky grey ottomans, boxy tables and marble floors) could squeeze in as many hip young things as it does on weekend nights. The rest of the time it's a great spot for a quiet glass of wine and tapas by the fireplace.
☎ 0486 42 07 10
✉ Emiel Banningstraat 15
🕑 2pm-late

Buster (8, B2)
This lively bar near the Grote Markt offers live jazz on most weeknights, including open jam sessions (on Thursdays) and gigs by jazz students from the Conservatorium of Antwerp and Jazz Studio (on Tuesdays and Wednesdays) – make an effort to catch one of these and bet to see who'll be a jazz great of the future. On Saturday there's stand-up comedy.
☎ 03 232 51 53
✉ Kaasrui 1 🕑 8pm to late, Mon-Fri

De Muze (8, B2)
The friendly service and jovial mood at this high-ceilinged stone pub make it a great place for a beer at any time, but it's especially fun when there's live jazz on, Monday to Saturday at 10pm, and 3pm on Sundays.
☎ 03 226 01 26 ✉ Melkmarkt 15 🕑 noon-2am

De Quinten Matsijs (8, C2)
This atmospheric traditional pub is Antwerp's oldest, dating to 1565. It gets crammed with locals at weekends, who come for the Trappist beers and traditional pub grub, especially the soup. Highly recommended.
☎ 03 225 01 70
✉ Moriaanstraat 17
🕑 noon-late Tue-Sat, noon-8pm Sun

Catch some jazz at Buster

FOR MEDICINAL PURPOSES ONLY

Jenever (also spelled as *genever*) is a juniper-flavoured liquor first sold as a medicinal nip in the 16th century because of its apparent 'health-giving' properties. The precursor to modern-day gin, it's still very popular in Flanders as well as other regions in this part of Europe. Running with an alcohol content of 38% to 43%, there are *jonge* (young) and *oude* (old) *jenevers* – which is more about the style of *jenever* than the ageing process. It's a great tipple on a cold winter's day – head straight to De Vagant (below) to savour its delights, sorry, medicinal properties.

De Vagant (8, B3)

This atmospheric *jenever* bar is the place to head to sip Belgian gin. If more than 200 on the menu make the choice too daunting, opt for the weekly blackboard special, the Oud Antwerpsche Cuvée Prestige (our favourite) or an exotic lychee, passionfruit or apple *jenever* (around €2.75 per shot). The delightful bar cat curls up on your lap at no extra charge.
☎ 03 233 15 38 ✉ Reyndersstraat 25 ◷ noon-late

Den Engel (8, B2)

A beer in this guildhall bar is obligatory, as is jostling with locals and tourists alike

De Muze (p87)

to get to the bar of what must be Antwerp's rowdiest pub. Despite being firmly on the tourist trail, it still has enough atmosphere to make a De Koninck or two here worthwhile.
☎ 03 233 12 52 ✉ Grote Markt 5 ◷ 9am-late

Hopper

While this small Zuid bar hosts some great names in jazz, the crowd it crams in can be a rather pretentious lot for Antwerp. We prefer the light airy space for a quiet afternoon drink – when it's empty – and prefer jazz at De Muze.
☎ 03 248 49 33 ✉ Leopold de Waelstraat 2 ◷ 10.30am-late, jazz 9pm Mon & Wed & 4pm Sun; € for decent jazz names on Wed €8, free on other nights

La Suite

A light, airy, low-key place by day, this bar goes off at night when the lights are down low, and although it's hard to squeeze through the door, it's worth it to soak up the crazy atmosphere.
☎ 0475 37 05 55 ✉ Luikstraat 9 ◷ 7.30am-3am Mon-Fri, 6pm-3am Sat

Lux

While some simply love the chic restaurant, others loathe its flamboyance, preferring instead to head straight for the stylish wine bar, or the funky club-style bar with its citrus ottomans, tangerine lighting and funky music.
☎ 03 233 30 30 ✉ Adriaan Brouwerstraat 13 ◷ 11am-1am Mon-Fri, 6pm-2am Sat

Mogador

While this was one of the first of Antwerp's cool contemporary bars, both the design and atmosphere of Mogador still hold up well. It's a stylish place for a cocktail on a cold winter's night, or a great place to kick back with a beer on the funky terrace outside during summer.
☎ 03 238 71 60 ✉ Graaf Van Egmontstraat 57 ◷ 5pm-late

Raga (8, C2)

This intimate red-walled wine bar on the wonderful square by St-Carolus-Borromeuskerk plays smooth jazz sounds and has serious wines by the glass. We can't

Cosy Raga (opposite)

resist their sparkling wine and oysters.

☎ 03 485 66 56 ✉ Hendrik Conscienceplein 11 ☾ 2pm-late Mon & Wed-Fri, noon-late Sat & Sun

't Elfde Gebod (8, B2)

The cosy 'Eleventh Com-mandment' is best visited in winter when it's popular with locals warming up on icy nights and there's barely a foreigner in sight. In summer, it gets crowded with tourists taking photos of its whimsical interior decorated with angels and other religious trinkets.

☎ 03 232 36 11 ✉ Torf-brug 10 ☾ noon-late

Zuiderterras (8, A3)

Once this bright airy space, with its terrace bar and stunning river views, was the only place on the water where you could have a drink. While more bar-restaurants have since appeared in the redeveloped docks areas, this is still one of the best spots to sip something on a sunny summer afternoon.

☎ 03 234 12 75 ✉ Ernest Van Dijckkaai 37 ☾ 11am-midnight

CLUBS

Café au Lait (8, B2)

This African-themed bar-club was started by a good-hearted mixed-race guy who wanted a club where black and white people could dance – it fills with locals here to boogie to Afro-funk most nights, rare '70s grooves on Sugar Sundays, and reggae, ska and soul on Tuesday.

☎ 03 225 19 81 ✉ Oude Beurs 8 ☾ 6pm-late Mon-Sat & 8pm-late Sun

Café d'Anvers

Located right in the heart of Antwerp's red-light supermarket, this legendary dance venue of 15 years is still attracting clubbers from far and wide for its top Belgian and international DJs spinning house (which is what the place is famous for), garage, funk, soul and disco, depending on the night – and they're all big nights!

☎ 03 226 38 70 ✉ Verversrui 15 ☾ 11pm-6am Thu, 11pm-7.30am Fri & Sat, 11pm-7.30am 1st Mon of month

Pier 19

While the food at the stylish restaurant downstairs is worth trying, it's the minimalist bar-club with its moody purple lighting and cool music that pulls the locals in.

☎ 03 288 78 61 ✉ Brouwersvliet 19 ☾ noon-3pm & 7-late Mon-Sat

Velvet Lounge (p90)

RED LIGHT SPECIAL

Antwerp's red-light district is Belgium's largest and opinions are sharply divided as to whether this is a good thing (in terms of containing violence and human trafficking) or simply makes Antwerp Belgium's biggest pimp. As part of a zone to control prostitution that was out of hand in the 1990s, the area – based around the Schipperskwartier (8, C1), or seaman's quarter – is now a controlled area for prostitution, with 24-hour police and a strict set of guidelines. The result is that the district is relatively safe for both the workers and the clients. On the ground, however, the result is that the girls on display in their shop fronts appear as commodified as a window display of a retail outlet on a shopping boulevard.

From dinner to dancing: you can spend all night at Stereo Sushi

Stereo Sushi
Antwerp's funkiest bar-club pulls in a hip crowd who snack on Asian tapas in the groovy space (chrome lamps, fluffy cushions, red Perspex Kartell chairs and Japanese manga murals). Come midnight it fills fast with clubbers keen to dance (Hed Kandi nights are particularly popular). The sultry **Velvet Lounge** restaurant-bar-club (upstairs) is worth a look.
☎ 03 248 67 27 ✉ Luikstraat 6 ⏱ 6pm-6am Wed-Sun, closed Jul & Aug

GAY & LESBIAN ANTWERP

Hessenhuis (8, D1)
In a wonderful historic building, this arts space, café, bar and club is home to Antwerp's gay crowd with DJs and dance events from Thursday to Sunday. The daily 9pm to 10pm happy hour keeps the place packed.
☎ 03 231 13 56 ✉ Falconrui 53 ⏱ 11am-late

Red & Blue
Antwerp's best gay club welcomes a mixed crowd on Fridays while Saturday is a harder core men's only night.
☎ 03 213 05 55 ✉ Lange Schipperskapelstraat 11-13 ⏱ 11pm-late Fri, 11am-7am Sat

CINEMA & THEATRE

Cartoon's
Antwerp's art house theatre shows some provocative world cinema and independent films in their original language.
☎ 03 232 96 32 ✉ Kaasstraat 4 ⏱ varies

De Singel
Head here for an adventurous programme of innovative theatre, classical music, modern dance, spoken word, live music, and architectural happenings.
☎ 03 248 28 28 🖳 www.desingel.be ✉ Desguinlei 25 ⏱ box office 10am-7pm Mon-Fri, 4-7pm Sat

Vlaamse Opera (8, E3)
Although the sumptuous interior of the 100-year-old Flemish Opera House is excuse enough to see a performance here, it's also home to the impressive Koninklijke Vlaamse Opera (Royal Flemish Opera).
☎ 03 233 66 85 ✉ Frankrijklei 3 ⏱ varies

Cartoon's: all the art house films you can handle

TOP END

De Witte Lelie (8, C2)

Housed in three restored 17th-century canal houses, the White Lily is the most refined hotel in town. With just 10 individually decorated rooms (with a brilliantly balanced mix of antique and modern), masses of fresh flowers, complementary liquors and fresh fruit and chocolate, along with the very discreet ambiance, it's bound to make your stay in Antwerp special. A class act.
☎ 03 226 19 66
🖳 www.dewittelelie.be
✉ Keizerstraat 16-18 ✂

Hotel Julien (8, C2)

Set within two restored townhouses, this is a contemporary, understated property in an excellent location near the Grote Markt. With only 11 rooms, it's a very private hotel and the details – such as a DVD/CD library and afternoon tea – make you feel right at home.
☎ 03 229 06 00
🖳 www.hotel-julien .com ✉ Korte Nieuwstraat 24 ✂

't Sandt (8, A3)

While this hotel has been somewhat over hyped by reviewers, it's a pleasant hotel with a lovely garden and some excellent suites, such as the Cathedral Penthouse (room 401). It's well positioned, but the attention to detail doesn't match that of De Witte Lelie (above).
☎ 03 232 93 90
🖳 www.hotel-sandt.be
✉ Zand 13-19 ✂

Time Out

Another of Antwerp's excellent B&Bs, this one features three rooms that are decorated by colour: Red, Purple and Blue. The blue room is slightly smaller than the other two but features a sun terrace, and all rooms are well equipped with a hi-fi, DVD player, wi-fi and tea-making facilities. While it's well-positioned for the galleries, bars and restaurants, it's quite a distance to the Grote Markt. It's also a nonsmoking B&B.
☎ 0498 12 37 73 🖳 www .timeout-antwerpen.be
✉ Tolstraat 49 ✂

MIDRANGE

Guesthouse 26 (8, B3)

This B&B is well positioned on a street filled with eccentric eateries near the Grote Markt and the style of the seven rooms here fits in well. The rooms are spacious, clean and feature some funky furnishings and extravagant touches. Some rooms have private bathrooms, while others are shared and there are triples

Guesthouse 26

available as well. Ask for a room in advance if you want a kitchenette.
☎ 0497 42 83 69 🖳 www .guesthouse26.com ✉ Pelgrimstraat 26

Hotel Antigone (8, B1)

Located on the water near Dock's Café (p84) and the maritime museum, most rooms here feature fine views of the Scheldt river. While the bedroom colour scheme won't please everyone (especially the green, red and yellow bed covers), the place is excellent value for money and they have

Stylish Slapenzeno (p92)

singles, triples and suites as well as doubles.
☎ 03 231 66 77
🖳 www.antigonehotel.be
✉ Jordaenskaai 11-12

Hotel Prinse (8, D2)
Situated in a lovely 16th-century building, this four-star has a modish reception and a lovely formal garden courtyard. The rooms don't quite live up to (or match) the surroundings, but they're spacious and well-maintained. All sights are an easy walk away.
☎ 03 226 40 50 🖳 www.hotelprinse.be ✉ Keizerstraat 63 ✗ ⚐ ⚐

Ibis Antwerpen Centrum
While everyone pretty much knows what to expect from an Ibis, the surprise here is the decent location, close to Rubenshuis (p78) and some decent shopping.
☎ 03 231 88 30
🖳 www.ibishotels.com
✉ Meistraat 39 ⚐

Le Patio (8, B2)
A beautifully detailed B&B, Le Patio offers three immaculate rooms with an almost country-cottage feel about them, courtesy of the owner's immaculate taste. The endearing rooms are spacious, individually decorated, and all have TV and wi-fi. The pleasant owner speaks only a little English.
☎ 03 232 76 61
🖳 www.lepatio.be
✉ Pelgrimstraat 8 ✗

Slapenenzo
Right at home in the fashion, art and nightlife district, this hip boutique hotel offers a series of rooms of different configurations and colours (black

Le Patio's simple country style

or white, thanks) – but with contemporary style being the common thread throughout. Lovely linen, Aqua di Parma bath and shower products, wi-fi and personal service make this a welcome addition to Antwerp's accommodation scene.
☎ 03 229 06 00 🖳 www.slapenenzo.be ✉ Korte Nieuwstraat 24 ✗ ✗

BUDGET

B&B Enich Anders (8, B3)
Run by a sweet (if slightly eccentric) sculptor who has her showroom downstairs, this B&B is a good choice for those who want the convenience of having a refrigerator and kitchenette as well as a great position near the Grote Markt. The rooms are simple, spacious and quiet and breakfast is a do-it-yourself number as ingredients are hung on your door for you early each morning. Nicotine addicts be aware that this is a nonnegotiable nonsmoking address.
☎ 03 231 37 92 🖳 enich.anders@antwerpen.be ✉ Leeuwenstraat 12 ✗ ⚐

Rubenshof
A quaint hotel set in a former cardinal's residence, the 22 rooms unfortunately don't really live up to the expectations drawn from the charming public spaces (especially the breakfast room). There's a choice of rooms with or without bathroom and all rooms are kept spotless and, while it's an invigorating 15 minutes' walk to the Grote Markt, it's handy to Antwerp's art galleries and nightlife.
☎ 03 237 07 89
🖳 www.rubenshof.be
✉ Amerikalei 115

B&B Enich Anders

While Antwerp is affluent today, its fortunes have waxed and waned over the centuries. Settled as early as the second century, Antwerp had become prosperous through its port and wool industries by the fourteenth century, and during the reign of King Charles V (ending in 1555) the city was a bustling metropolis. In 1566, after the Protestants destroyed the city's cathedral in the Iconoclastic Fury, Spanish King Philip II sent in the troops, but 10 years later these underpaid troops staged what is known as the Spanish Fury – killing around 8000 locals. The Spanish were driven out, returning in 1585 with Philip II ordering Antwerp to become a Catholic city – which prompted an exodus of inhabitants to the United Provinces (today's Netherlands). The Scheldt river was closed in 1648 to all non-Dutch ships and the city shrank in importance until 1797, when Napoleon arrived and rebuilt the docks. Through all this time Antwerp's cultural life has been vibrant – from the 17th-century paintings of Peter Paul Rubens (p77) to today's fashion design of the Antwerp 6 (p80).

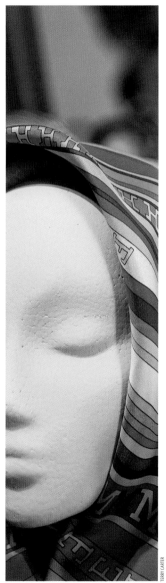

Mode Museum (MoMu, p77)

VLAAMS BLOK & VLAAMS BELANG

The political party Vlaams Belang (Flemish Interest) was formed in 2004 by members of the Vlaams Blok (Flemish Block) party which was banned after the High Court ruled that it was inciting discrimination and racism. This far right party, running on policies including independence for Flanders and strict immigration limitations, is currently the largest party in Flemish Parliament. But due to a *cordon sanitaire* (where other parties refuse to join a coalition with it), it remains out of power.

While Antwerp and Bruges steal the limelight with their arty vibe and picture-postcard vistas respectively, Ghent (Gent in Flemish and Gand in French) is content being a mostly undiscovered gem – for about 50 weeks of the year, that is. In mid-July, a big multicultural festival, the Gentse Feesten (for more information see www.gentsefeesten.be), turns Ghent's pretty city centre into a dedicated, hedonistic party zone, with international DJs, plenty of beer drinking and street theatre.

Gravensteen (p96)

Visit Ghent at any other time of the year – minus the alcoholic haze that accompanies the festival – and you'll find a city with a buzzy student scene that's full of wonderful Flemish architecture, atmospheric canals and a great range of hotels, eateries and bars that are as hip or traditional as you could wish for.

The city doesn't want for art and history either. Sights such as the Gravensteen, a formidable 12th-century medieval castle, is a short stroll away from St-Baafskathedraal with one of the world's great art treasures, Jan Van Eyck's stunning 20-panel altarpiece, *Adoration of the Mystic Lamb*. And while Ghent was, during mediaeval times, the biggest city in Europe outside Paris, it's not all history. The Design Museum and Museum of Fine Arts (SMAK) highlight a city that's dramatic and wilful. It's a city that marches to the beat of its own drum – and it's a compelling rhythm.

Het Waterhuis aan de Bierkant is just a short stagger away from 't Dreupelkot (p99)

Ghent's lovely **historic heart** is centred on mighty St-Baafskathedraal and the Belfort (belfry) which are surrounded by cobblestone streets and what Ghent proudly claims to be the largest pedestrian area in all of Europe. However, as the deadly push-bikes have right of way and seem to come at you from every angle, you often feel it would be safer with roads!

To the north of St-Baafskathedraal is the Vrijdagmarkt with its morning food markets, outdoor cafés and stylish boutiques. The cobblestone lanes of the charming **Patershol** area in the north west, on the other side of the Leie canal, is a joy to explore, as is its imposing Gravensteen castle.

Across the canal again is a quaint area that's home to the design museum and some fascinating shops. The Korenlei is the open pedestrian area that runs along this side of the canal, looking across to the Graslei on the other side. These offer stunning views, especially at night, when the splendid guild houses and bridges are superbly lit, and there are some great pubs and bars from which to enjoy them! This is also where the boats dock for canal cruises. South of here from St-Michielsbrug (bridge) you get the most wondrous views of all of the three towers: those of St-Niklaaskerk, St-Baafskathedraal and the Belfort.

> **OFF THE BEATEN TRACK**
> • Feed the ducks before enjoying some art in low-key Citadelpark
> • Wander along the canalside on Coupure Links and Coupure Rechts, where you can watch student rowing teams on weekend mornings

Reflections on one of Ghent's canalways

Across the canal again, south of St-Niklaaskerk is Ghent's main commercial area, with all the high street franchises you find in any city around the world, getting ritzier the further south you go, especially approaching Zonnestraat and the Vogelmarkt, home to the theatre district.

On the other side of the Ketelvaart canal, across both Ketelbrug and Walpoortbrug bridges, you will find a large area that's home to Ghent's enormous student population. Around the Walpoortbrug are some excellent CD stores, skate shops, second-hand clothes stores, avant garde theatres and music venues. Further south along St-Pietersnieuwstraat and Overpoortstraat are scores of grungy student bars, busy most evenings, but absolutely packed on Thursday nights before the students go home for the weekend.

Belfort (7, B2)

The bells of Ghent's 14th-century belfry tower warned of enemy invasions and announced executions and important visitors to the city. You'll just be welcomed with spectacular views.

☎ 09 233 07 72 ⊠ Emile Braunplein € €2.50/1 ☼ 10am-12.30pm & 2-5.30pm Easter-Nov

Gravensteen (7, A1)

This majestic 12th-century Castle of the Counts has an absorbing weapons museum with some exquisitely detailed cross-bows, pistols and powder horns, and a gruesome display of torture devices offset by awesome views.

☎ 09 225 93 06 ⊠ St-Veerleplein € €2.50 ☼ 9am-6pm Apr-Sep, 9am-5pm Oct-Mar

Huis van Alijn (7, B1)

This delightful Museum of Things That Never Pass leads you through displays of curiosities from popular culture and everyday life themed around love, pain, faith, passion, death…

☎ 09 269 23 50 ⊠ Kraanlei 65 € €2.50/1.20 ☼ 11am-5pm Tue-Sat, 10am-5pm Sun

Museum voor Schone Kunsten

With the museum closed for renovation until 2007, many of the Fine Arts Museum's masterpieces can instead be seen in the crypt of St-Baafskathedraal, and rotating exhibitions at the **Museumpaviljoen** (Charles de Kerchovelaan 187a).

☎ 09 240 07 00 ⊠ Citadelpark € €2.50/1.20 ☼ 10am-6pm Tue-Sun

Museum voor Vormgeving (7, A2)

This fascinating Design Museum exhibits everything from wonderful Art Nouveau and Art Deco decorative arts from the likes of Horta and Le Corbusier to Ron Arad's 1994 stainless steel sofa.

☎ 09 267 99 99 ⊠ Jan Breydelstraat 5 € €2.50/1.20 ☼ 10am-6pm Tue-Sun

St-Baafskathedraal (7, C2)

Late-Gothic St Bavo's Cathedral has some impressive art, including Rubens' *Entry of St Bavo into the Monastery* and masterpieces from the Museum voor Schone Kunsten, including Bosch' grotesque *Christ Carrying the Cross*, however, head straight

Pulpit at St-Baafskathedraal

for the Van Eyck brothers' vibrant altarpiece **Adoration of the Mystic Lamb** (admission €3 incl audio guide; ☼ 9.30am-5pm Mon-Sat, 1-4.30pm Sun Apr-Oct, 10.30am-3.45pm Mon-Sat, 1-3.30pm Sun Nov-Mar).

☎ 09 269 20 45 ⊠ St-Baafsplein ☼ 8.30am-6pm

Stedelijk Museum voor Actuele Kunst/SMAK (7, C3)

Get your contemporary art fix at SMAK, one of the country's most provocative museums, with a permanent collection including internationals such as Joseph Beuys and Belgian stars such as Luc Tuymans and Panamarenko.

☎ 09 221 17 03 ⊠ Citadelpark € €5/3.80, 10am-1pm Sun free ☼ 10am-6pm Tue-Sun

GHENT VISTAS

Ghent has several vantage points from which to appreciate its graceful canals and guildhouses:

- Belfort (7, B2) – sweeping views of Ghent's skyline
- Korenlei (7, A2) – postcard views of Graslei
- Gravensteen (7, A1) – step-gabled guildhouses and church steeples
- Sint Michielsbrug (7, A2) – the three towers: St-Niklaaskerk, the Belfort (pictured) and St-Baafskathedraal

Atlas & Zanzibar (7, C3)
Here, in one of the best travel-book shops in Belgium, if not the world, you'll find an enormous range of travel guides (including Lonely Planet), along with travel literature, in English, French and Dutch, plus maps, globes, videos, CD-roms, and calendars.
☎ 09 220 87 99 ✉ Kortrijksesteenweg 19 ⏱ 10am-1pm & 2-6.30pm Mon-Fri, 10am-6pm Sat

Fallen Angels (7, A2)
For an original souvenir, take some time to browse these two whimsical shops, ran by a mother and daughter, specialising in Belgian kitsch and collectables – wonderful old postcards, posters, tin boxes, signs, ashtrays, snow domes and old-fashioned toys, such as delicate old dolls, toy trains, and tin robots.
☎ 09 223 94 15, 225 17 71 ✉ Jan Breydelstraat 29-31, ⏱ 1-6pm Wed-Sat & Mon

Groot Vleeshuis (7, B2)
In this wonderful old meat market, dating back to the Middle Ages, you can taste delicious regional products,

and if you like what you try, buy them. Head across the road to **Tierenteijn-Verlent** (7, B2; ☎ 09 225 83 36) at number 3 for mustards made here since 1790.
☎ 09 267 86 07 ✉ Groentenmarkt 7 ⏱ 10am-6pm Tue-Sun

Het Oorcussen (7, B1)
Blink and you might miss this understated Vrijdagmarkt store stocking the best Belgian women's fashion designers – Dries Van Noten, Ann Demeulemeester, Martin Margiela, Veronique Branquinho, Isabelle Baines etc, and jewellery designer Karin Nunez de Fleurquin. Around the corner, the brother of the store's owner runs **Obius** (7, B1; ☎ 09 233 82 69; Meerseniersstraat 4; ⏱ 10.30am-6.30pm Tue-Sat, 1.30-6.30pm Mon), specialising in men's wear and shoes by the same designers.
☎ 09 233 07 65 ✉ Vrijdagmarkt 7 ⏱ 10.30am-6pm Tue-Sat, 1.30-6pm Mon

Home Linen (7, A2)
For the old-fashioned souls inside us all, a splendid

Colourful Zsa Zsa Rouge

selection of hand-made linens (sheets, towels, night-gowns) along with heavenly lavender products (handmade soaps, room mist, pillow spray) and the kind of antique jewellery that you found on grandma's dressing table (wonderful lockets, jewelled watches and eternity rings).
☎ 09 223 60 93 ✉ Korenlei 3 ⏱ 10am-6pm

Zoot (7, B2)
This hip little shop specialises in vintage and groovy retro-like gear created by young designers.
☎ 09 233 7075
✉ Serpentstraat 8
⏱ 11am-6.30pm Tue-Sat, 2-6.30pm Mon

Zsa Zsa Rouge (7, B2)
There's lots of irresistible, colourful and crazy stuff in Zsa Zsa Rouge, an eccentric lifestyle store, and **Petit Zsa Zsa** (7, B2; Serpentstraat 5; ☎ 09 224 4574), a quirky kids clothes and toy store, in the same lane as Zoot.
☎ 09 225 93 63
✉ Serpentstraat 22

Brasserie HA' (7, B3)

Contemporary Belgian €€
This modish eatery serves up refined brasserie food in a lovely airy space with high ceilings and wooden floors. The food is a notch above most brasserie fare with inventive touches throughout the menu – the fish and meat mains are excellent.
☎ 09 265 91 81 🖳 www .brasserieha.be ✉ Kouter 29 🕑 noon-2.30pm Tue-Sun & 6-10pm Tue-Sat 🔅

Brasserie Pakhuis (7, B2)

French/Italian €€
Located in a fantastic restored warehouse, a visit to this brasserie is compulsory – even if it's just for a drink. However the food is worth staying for, especially for the brasserie staples including excellent oysters and shellfish.
☎ 09 223 55 55 🖳 www .pakhuis.be ✉ Schuurken-straat 4 🕑 11.30am-1am Mon-Thu & 11.30am-2am Fri & Sat Ⓥ

De Blauwe Zalm (7, B1)

French/seafood €€€
Ask a local foodie what the best seafood restaurant is in town and they'll invariably point you to this elegant seafood restaurant (opposite Karel de Stoute). And with good reason: the food is fresh, refined and exquisitely presented.
☎ 09 224 08 52 ✉ Vrouwe-broersstraat 2 🕑 noon-1.30pm Tue-Fri & 7-9pm Mon-Sat

Du Progrès (7, B2)

Traditional Belgian €€
This centrally located, casual brasserie is filled with locals

Brasserie HA': contemporary brasserie fare with a twist

here for the tender cuts of meat and fantastic sauces (delicious Béarnaise!) and outsized servings of vege-tables and home-style mash. Delicious home-style pastas as well.
☎ 09 225 17 16 🖳 www .duprogres.be ✉ Koren-markt 10 🕑 8am-midnight Thu-Mon 🔅

Karel de Stoute (7, B1)

Modern French/Belgian €€€
Skilfully run by a young couple, this elegant, contem-porary restaurant is a class act. From the *amuse bouche* to the petit fours, the food is a sensory delight. Chef Lode Ryckaert has trained with some great Belgian chefs – and it shows.
☎ 09 224 17 35 🖳 www .resto.com/kareldestoute in Dutch & French ✉ Vrouwebroersstraat 5 🕑 noon-1.30pm Tue-Sat & 6.30-10pm Mon-Sat

Keizershof (7, B1)

Belgian brasserie €€
Located right on the market square, this buzzy, informal eatery serves up traditional Ghent favourites in a contemporary setting. Order the much-loved dishes, such as the Trappist beer beef

stew – but only if you're famished, as portions are huge.
☎ 09 223 44 46 🖳 www .keizershof.net in Dutch & French ✉ Vrijdagmarkt 47 🕑 noon-2.30pm & 6pm-22.30 Tue-Sat 🔅

Souplounge (7, B1)

Soup €
Friendly, fast and funky, this soup kitchen keeps the locals happy with its selection of four daily soups, all of which come with your choice of garnishes as well as bread, butter and a piece of fruit.
☎ 09 223 62 03 ✉ Zuivel-brugstraat 6 🕑 10am-7pm Ⓥ 🔅

Souplounge

Belga Queen (7, B2)

This atmospheric space in a 13th-century grain storehouse on the beautiful Graslei is the creation of visionary chef-entrepreneur Antoine Pinto (behind Brussels' Belga Queen, p35, Ghent's Pakhuis, opposite, and Antwerp's Dock's Café, p84). With its bare brick walls and chandeliers, it's part restaurant, tearoom, oyster bar, cigar bar and club, with live music and DJs from Thursday through weekends.
☎ 09 280 01 00 ✉ Graslei 10 ⏱ noon-midnight

Café Theatre (7, B3)

Spread over two levels, this stylish, clubby bar, with red walls and comfy seats, is a great place for some bubbly, especially on a winter's day when it's cosy inside. There's a good brasserie next door.
☎ 09 265 05 50 ✉ Schouwburgstraat 5 ⏱ noon-late

Culture Club

This übercool club with very cool mood lighting is considered to be one of Europe's best, hosting the hottest DJs most Friday and Saturday nights. Check the online programme before trekking out of town.
☎ 09 233 09 46
🖥 www.cultureclub.be

✉ Afrikalaan 174
⏱ 11pm-early Fri & Sat

Het Waterhuis aan de Bierkant (7, B1)

Popular for its wide range of beers on tap, this traditional, smoky, canal-side pub gets buzzy with locals at night. When you've had your fill of beer, pop next door to **'t Dreupelkot** (☎ 09 224 21 20) to try some *jenever* (Belgian gin).
☎ 09 225 06 80 ✉ Groentenmarkt 9, ⏱ 11am-late

Limonada (7, B2)

This cool-looking space fills up quickly when the doors open with locals eager to grab a beanbag and sink in to sip some cocktails at this funky laidback lounge bar.
☎ 09 233 78 85 ✉ Heilige Geeststraat 7 ⏱ 8pm-late Mon-Sat

Pink Flamingoes (7, B2)

This eccentric bar, decorated with ever-changing kitsch – including some far out window displays – gets crowded with locals who settle in for the night. If you like it here, also try retro-looking cocktail bar, **Gainsbar** (7, B1; ☎ 09 225 1969; Oudburg 51).

Café Theatre

☎ 09 233 47 18 ✉ Onderstraat 55 ⏱ noon-midnight Mon-Wed, 2pm-3am Thu-Sat

Vooruit

This alternative performance, theatre, arts and cultural space – hosting everything from jazz to flamenco, and book-readings to lectures – was once a socialist party cultural centre and still has a very bo-ho left-wing feel about it. The atmospheric foyer bar is a great place to stop for coffee or drinks.
☎ 09 267 28 20 🖥 www .vooruit.be ✉ St-Pietersnieuwstraat 23 ⏱ 11.30am-late

Relax in one of Limonada's beanbags

TOP END

Hotel Cour St-Georges
(7, B2)
Situated in a wonderful 18th-century building, this is the oldest hotel in Ghent, and said to be one of the oldest hotels in Europe. The breakfast room is gorgeous, but only one suite remains in the old style, with the rest being business-like.
☎ 09 224 24 24 🖳 www .bestwestern.be/residence stgeorges ✉ Hoogpoort 75 ♿ fair

Hotel de Flandre (7, A2)
This renovation of an old building in a contemporary style makes for a very pleasant hotel with warm modern lighting and dark wooden furniture. The loft rooms are great with fabulous skylights and cherry wooden furniture, while the suites really impress – enormous with DVD, flat screen TVs, big fireplaces, giant bathroom and sitting area.
☎ 09 266 06 00 🖳 www.hoteldeflandre.be ✉ Poel 1-2 ⊗ ♿ fair

Hotel de Flandre loft room

GHENT'S B&B BARGAINS
Ghent has a fantastic bed & breakfast scene, with rooms to suit all tastes and budgets – it's also a great way to get to know the particularly private Belgians. The easiest way to book is to use the excellent, no-nonsense website www.bedandbreakfast-gent.be.

MIDRANGE

Erasmus (7, A2)
This small and friendly hotel, housed in a restored 16th-century building, has plenty of medieval charm, particularly in its larger rooms. The hotel is in a good location, has wi-fi and a great buffet breakfast where a suit of armour watches your every move.
☎ 09 224 21 95 🖳 www.proximedia .com/web/hotel-erasmus .html ✉ Poel 25 ♿ fair

Hotel Harmony (7, B1)
This wonderful contemporary hotel, in two renovated old buildings (with a garden in between) on the canal, was lovingly restored by a husband and wife team who have fantastic attention to detail. Rooms 10 and 11 both have fantastic views and room 31 has great views as well as a large terrace.
☎ 09 324 26 80 🖳 www.hotel-harmony .be ✉ Kraanlei 37 ⊗ ⊠ 🏊 ♿ excellent

Ibis Gent Centrum St-Baafskathedraal (7, B2)
It's fair to say that the best thing about this hotel is the location – you can almost lean out of your window and touch St-Baafskathedraal from here – helping to take your mind off the old-school

Ibis rooms. Needless to say it's conveniently located for sightseeing and the hotel has wi-fi.
☎ 09 233 00 00 🖳 www .ibishotels.com ✉ Limburg-straat 2 ⊗ ♿ fair

Monasterium Poort Ackere (7, A3)
A former convent, these atmospheric digs boast a hotel section, with modern, well-furnished rooms, and the more austere guesthouse rooms. All have views of the garden, a TV and tea- and coffee-making facilities along with an excellent breakfast. There are small single rooms (with shared bathrooms) and the hotel has wi-fi.
☎ 09 269 22 10 🖳 www.monasterium.be ✉ Oude Houtlei 56 ⊗ ♿ fair

Stylish Hotel Harmony

Ghent has a long and industrious history and is one of Belgium's oldest cities, having much prominence in Europe between 1100 and 1500. By the late 13th century the city had become a major wool-producing centre, importing the wool from England, and most of the town was in some way involved in wool production, either as weavers, fullers, shearers and dyers – each with its own guild. These guilds were of great importance to Ghent, protecting workers rights as well as being politically active.

Charles V, one of the most important rulers in European history, was born in Ghent in 1500 and around 1540 he crushed a rebellion after the townsfolk refused to pay taxes. The subsequent punishment – being publicly humiliated by wearing a noose around the neck – earned them the nickname *Stropdragers* (noose wearers).

Over there! Vrijdagmarkt

Today Ghent is the capital of the province of Oost-Vlaanderen and is a vibrant university town. It has an overall population of just over half a million inhabitants, with around half that number living in the city area of Ghent itself. Its port, university, polytechnics and research and development centres as well as healthcare facilities are the main sources of income and employment.

As you would expect from a city with 45,000 students, there's a vibrant bar scene and underground art scene (not to mention the odd party or two!) and there's a disproportionate number of iPod-wearing, instrument carrying kids on the streets heading to an impromptu gig or to practice. SMAK (p96) offers up some challenging contemporary art that belies the living museum vibe of its cobbled streets.

It sure was fun in the Middle Ages; Gravensteen castle (p96)

WALKING TOURS
Atmospheric Amble in Brussels

A great introduction to Brussels, this amble takes in the most atmospheric spots and main sights but is really a bar (or café) hop in disguise. Providing plenty of opportunities to imbibe good Belgian beer, it's best started late afternoon or early evening. Start at gorgeous gilded **Café Métropole** (**1**; p43) on Place de Brouckère. Turn left onto Rue du Fossé-aux-Loups and right onto Place de la Monnaie, passing elegant **Théâtre Royal de la Monnaie** (**2**; p48). Turn left into Rue de l'Écuyer to **À la Mort Subite** (**3**; p43) for a beer of the same name, before doing

Not just for kids: Théâtre Royal de Toone

a lap of beautiful **Galeries Royales St-Hubert** (**4**; p28). Backtrack to the arcade's centre, heading into **Rue des Bouchers** (**5**; p24) to soak up the atmosphere of the neon-lit eat street. Take Petite Rue des Bouchers, and half way along stick your nose into faded **Théâtre Royal de Toone** (**6**; p25). Turn left into Rue du Marché-aux-Herbes and right into Rue des Hareings to arrive at the magnificent **Grand Place** (**7**; p8). Stroll around the square, sticking your head into convivial **'t Kelderke** (**8**; p36, you may want to eat here later), before stopping for a drink at **Roy d'Espagne** (**9**; p45).

Get a window seat to admire the splendid gabled architecture. Take Rue au Beurre and Rue de la Bourse to wonderful **Cirio** (**10**; p44) then around the corner to **Falstaff** (**11**; p44). Cross over to Rue Auguste Orts, to Art Deco **L'Archiduc** (**12**; p45) for some jazz over cocktails, then to **Fin de Siècle** (**13**; p44) for a well-deserved meal. After dinner, finish off at the Place St-Géry bars.

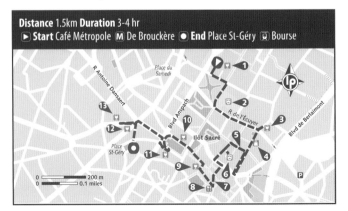

Distance 1.5km **Duration** 3-4 hr
▶ **Start** Café Métropole Ⓜ De Brouckère ● **End** Place St-Géry 🚊 Bourse

Brussels Mural Mosey

Check out the Centre Belge de la Bande Dessinée (p14) before the walk to get the most out of Brussels' street murals. Begin at Place St-Géry with Marc Sleen's popular character **Nero** (**1**) before taking Rue des Chartreux to see Yslaire's beautiful **L'Archange** (**2**). Continue along Rue

des Fabriques to Rue de la Senne for Bob de Moor's **Cori Le Moussaillon** (**3**) and Hermann's fantastical **The Dreams of Nic** (**4**). On Rue de la Senne, take the second left to view Morris' Western parody **Lucky Luke** (**5**). Continue down Rue de la Buanderie, turning right into Rue Van Artevelde, then left into Rue de la Verdure. At Place Anneessens is Willy Maltaite's beautiful **Isabelle** (**6**). Turn left into Blvd Maurice Lemonnier to visit second-hand book shop **Pêle-Mêle** (**7**; p32) for cheap comics, and dozens of specialist comic book shops, such as Brüsel (p32). Turn right into Rue du Bon Secours for Tibet's adventurous **Ric Hochet** (**8**) then left into Rue du Marché au Charbon for Francis Carin's suave spy **Victor Sackville** (**9**) and Frank Pe's **Broussaille** (**10**). Once at Rue Midi

Lucky Luke, faster than his shadow

(where you turn right) you'll see François Schuiten's **Le Passage** (**11**). Arriving at Rue des Grands Carmes, hang a left to see Dany's **Olivier Rameau** (**12**) and another little character, **Manneken Pis** (**13**; p22). Refuel at **Au Cercle des Voyageurs** (**14**; p43).

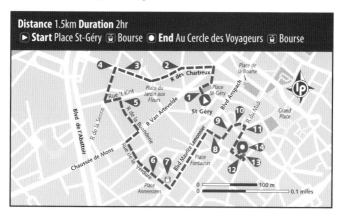

Distance 1.5km **Duration** 2hr
▶ **Start** Place St-Géry 🚇 Bourse ● **End** Au Cercle des Voyageurs 🚇 Bourse

Canalside Stroll in Bruges

Start your saunter along Bruges' canals at the **Burg** (**1**; p63). Cross Blinde Ezelstraat bridge, turn left on Steenhouwersdijk and stop at the **Vismarkt** (**2**; fish market). Stroll along charming Groenerei and at the end cross Predikherenbrug (bridge) for a lovely view. Continue along the waterfront

Distance 2km **Duration** 2½hr
▶ **Start** Burg ● **End** canal cruise

to the **Molenbrug** (**3**) pausing on this bridge for picturesque vistas. Walk along the Verversdijk, taking in the beautiful gabled buildings. Cross the second bridge, **Strooibrug** (**4**) at the canal junction for more stunning views before hitting Blekerstraat to Bruges' oldest pub, **Café Vlissinghe** (**5**; p70). After refreshments cross **Carmersbrug** (**6**) and stop for more scenic views and perhaps a swan or two. Follow Spiegelrei to **Jan Van Eyckplein** (**7**), with a statue of the artist, and walk across Biskajersplein to the Kraanrei, leading into Ieperstraat and Cordoeaniersstraat. Turn right into Philipstockstraat to the magnificent **Markt** (**8**; p64) and climb the **Belfort** (**9**; p64) for breathtaking vistas. Exit at the back, turning right into Oude Burg, left into Nieuwstraat, left into Gruuthusestraat, and walk along the **Dijver** (**10**) – one of Bruges' prettiest promenades. Lunch on the sun terrace at beer restaurant **Den Dyver** (**11**; p68), then head to **Rozenhoedkaai** (**12**) for the most gorgeous views of all. Turn into delightful **Huidenvettersplein** (**13**) and just before Blinde Ezelstraat bridge board a boat for a **canal cruise** (**14**; p108) to enjoy beautiful Bruges from another perspective – the canals themselves.

Brugge Blond, a popular lighter style beer

Fashion Flit through Antwerp

Begin a morning flit through Antwerp's fashionable streets at the flagship store of original Antwerp 6 (p80) designer **Ann Demeulemeester** (**1**; p79) on the corner of Verlatstraat and Volkstraat, before heading up Nationalestraat to the minimalist store of **Veronique Branquinho** (**2**; p80). Around the corner on St-Antoniusstraat is **Walter** (**3**; p80), flagship store of Antwerp 6 wild-man Walter Beirendonck whose fashion is political and provocative. Continue on St-Antoniusstraat and Oudaan to Lange Gasthuisstraat and chic **Verso** (**4**; p80) for Dirk Bikkembergs and Dirk Schönberger. Turn right to Schuttershofstraat and **Delvaux** (**5**; ☎ 03 232 02 47; Komedieplaats 17), Belgium's finest handbag maker, and **Coccodrillo** (**6**; p79) for shoes by Belgian designers. Backtrack to Korte Gasthuisstraat, head toward Lombardenvest, turn left and **Louis** (**7**; p80) is on your left, stockist of Antwerp designers Martin Margiela and AF Vandervorst among others. Continue to Kammenstraat to **Hit** (**8**; p81) for funky streetwear by Antwerp designers, then to Nationalestraat to **Het Modepaleis** (**9**; p79), the ornate flagship store of another Antwerp 6 designer, Dries Van Noten. Around the corner on Vrijdagmarkt is Belgian's best jewellery designer, **Christa Reniers**

Scarves galore at Mode Museum (MoMu)

(**10**; p79). Take Drukkerijstraat to fabulous **MoMu** (**11**; p77), the Mode Museum, for its latest exhibition, before browsing fashion books at **Copyright** (**12**; p82) and lunching at stylish **Brasserie National** (**13**; p83) – think of all the calories you've just burnt off!

Distance 1.75km **Duration** 2½hr
▶ **Start** Ann Demeulemeester ● **End** Brasserie Nationale

Get Traditional in Ghent

Spend some time at **St-Baafskathedraal** (**1**; p96) appreciating the sublime *Adoration of the Mystic Lamb* and masterpieces from the fine arts museum, then (if visiting in summer) climb up the **Belfort** (**2**; p96) for spec-

tacular views over the city. Walk by the beautiful **Stadhuis** (**3**; town hall) on Botermarkt, then along Hoogpoort to the **Groot Vleeshuis** (**4**; p97) to sample traditional regional foods. Head up Lange Munt to the **Vrijdagmarkt** (**5**) to see if there's a market on, then take Zuivelbrug-straat for pretty canal views from the **Zuivelbrug** (**6**; bridge). In the atmospheric quarter of Patershol, visit the charming **Huis van Alijn** (**7**; p96) folklore museum, and enjoy another gorgeous view from the **Kraanlei** (**8**), before exploring the backstreets (packed with restaurants) and heading to **Gravensteen castle** (**9**; p96) for its grisly torture and weapons museums and a great outlook over the city, then cross the Hoofdbrug and continue along

Imposing Gravensteen castle

WAYNE WALTON

cobblestone Jan Breydelstraat to the **Korenlei** (**10**) for good views of the gabled guildhouses across the canal. Take the stairs up to **St-Michielsbrug** (**11**) for the best vistas yet of the three towers – St-Niklaaskerk, the Belfort and St-Baafskathedraal. Finish with a traditional meal at **Du Progrès** (**12**; p98) on the Korenmarkt followed by a local beer at **Het Waterhuis aan de Bierkant** (**13**; p99) and **'t Dreupelkot** (**14**; p99) for a *jenever* (Belgian gin).

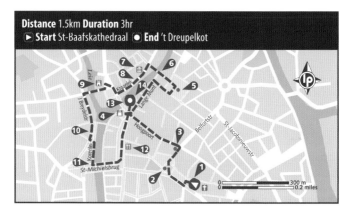

Distance 1.5km **Duration** 3hr
▶ **Start** St-Baafskathedraal ● **End** 't Dreupelkot

ORGANISED TOURS

Brussels

ARAU (3, D2)

This urban heritage group, Atelier de Recherche et d'Action Urbaines (Work-shop for Town-Planning Research & Action), runs theme tours on Art Deco, Art Nouveau, suburban growth etc, and focused on different areas.

☎ 02 219 33 45
🖥 www.arau.org ✉ Blvd Adolphe Max 55, Lower Town
€ walking tour €10; coach tour €15 ⏱ tours 10am or 2pm Sat & Sun Apr-Nov

Brussels by Water (3, C1)

While not as attractive as the canals of Ghent or Bruges, the Brussels canals are nevertheless interesting to those who like to take to water. Brussels by Water offers a number of tours; check the website for their many offerings.

☎ 02 203 64 06
🖥 www.scaldisnet.be

See the sights in an Open Tours bus

✉ Ave du Port, Lower Town
€ from €6/5

Open Tours (4, F6)

These open-roofed double-decker buses depart from Gare Centrale for a 90-minute tour of the city.

☎ 02 466 11 11 🖥 www.open-tours.com ✉ Gare Centrale, Upper Town
€ €12-20 ⏱ hourly from 10am

Pro Velo (3, F5)

Most of Pro Velo's themed bike tours around various parts of the city are three to four hours long, although you can also do self-guided tours.

☎ 02 502 73 55 🖥 www.provelo.org ✉ Rue de Londres 15, Upper Town
€ tours from €8

Visit Brussels Line (4, E5)

This double-decker bus does a variety of tours, including Brussels discovery tours, city trips and hop-on-hop-off tours, which depart Gare Centrale for a circuit of 14 key city attractions and is valid for 24 hours.

☎ 02 513 77 44 🖥 www.brussels-city-tours.com
✉ Rue de la Colline 8,

Pretty Dijver lit up at night, with St-Salvatorskathedraal (p64) in the background, Bruges

Happy chappies on the façade of Stadhuis (p63) in Bruges

Lower Town € hop-on-hop-off from €16/8/14.50 ⏰ every 30min 10am-4pm Mon-Fri, 10am-5pm Sat

Bruges
Canal Cruises (1, C5 & D4)
One of the most popular activities in Bruges are canal tours. While they're very touristy, they're also very lovely. Several companies run boats from docks on the Dijver, Rozenhoedkaai and by the Blinde Ezelstraat bridge.
✉ Dijver, Rozenhoedkaai & Blinde Ezelstraat € €6/3 ⏰ every 20 min 10am-6pm Feb-Nov

Horse-Dawn Carriage (1, D3)
Long lines of tourists fill the Markt throughout the day, patiently waiting their turn for a horse-drawn tour of historical Bruges, with a woolly blanket on their laps in winter.
✉ Markt € per carriage €30 ⏰ 9am-early evening, depending on demand

Quasimundo (1, E3)
This company offers bike tours exploring the Bruges

backstreets, Bruges by night rides and bike trips to the Dutch border (€60).
☎ 050 33 07 75 🖥 www.quasimundo.be ✉ meeting point Toyo Ito pavilion near the Burg ⏰ 10am-12.45pm Mar-Oct € €20

Antwerp
Antwerp Diamond Bus (8, F3)
The blue hop-on-hop-off open-roofed double-decker buses depart from Centraal Station near the Diamond Museum for a one-hour trip around the city (with

audio tour on headphones in eight languages), making seven stops at key sights such as the Groenplaats, the Royal Museum of Fine Arts, St-Michielskaai and Steenplein, before returning to the Diamond District. They also offer combined harbour and city tours.
☎ 03 513 77 44, 0478 48 28 20 € valid 24hr €11/6/10 ⏰ hourly from 10.30am, last bus at 4.30pm, daily Apr-Oct, Sat & Sun Nov-Mar

Bike Tours (8, B2)
The Tourism Information Office of the Province of

On ya bike – it's a great way to get around

RICK GERHARTER

Ferrying tourists around Bruges the old-school way

Antwerp in the Grote Markt has detailed maps with bicycle routes based on themes (architecture, Rubens and so on) or by area, so you can do a self-guided tour and discover the city by bike, or the tourism office can organise a guide. Rent your bike first – see p112.
☎ 03 232 01 03
✉ Grote Markt 13
€ per hr/day €3/12
☼ 9am-5.45pm Mon-Sat, 9am-4.45pm Sun

Daems Horse & Carriage (8, B2)
Ride a horse-drawn carriage through the historic centre of the city, departing from the Grote Markt in front of the Stadhuis, frequently in fine weather, but in winter it's weather-dependent.
☎ 0475 74 66 20
✉ Grote Markt
€ 10/20min €10/19
☼ noon-6pm daily Jul & Aug, Sat & Sun Sep-Jun, weather-permitting Nov-Mar

Flandria (8, A2)
Take a 50-minute (depart-ing from the Steenplein) or

2½-hour (from 't Eilandje) Scheldt river excursion. Flandria also offers evening cruises and day trips to Zeebrugge, Oostende and other locations, from March to October only.
☎ 03 231 31 00
▱ www.flandriaboat.com
✉ Steenplein
€ from €8/6

Ghent
Canal Cruises (7, A2)
Like Bruges, Ghent has some very pretty canals and seeing the city from the water offers a different perspective. Two companies operate canal cruises, Gent Watertoerist and De Bootjes van Gent, situated just west of the Korenmarkt.
☎ Gent Watertoerist 09 266 05 22; De Bootjes van Gent 09 223 88 53
✉ Graslei & Korenlei
€ Gent Watertoerist (40 min) €4.50/2.25, De Bootjes van Gent (90 min) €9/4.50 ☼ frequent depar-tures in summer, dependent on weather and numbers in winter

Kroegentocht (7, A2)
If a bar hop by boat (covered and heated in winter) takes your fancy – guided by a town crier – you must try this one out. Most people love it. The boat stops at Ghent's best pubs and the cruise includes an entertain-ing commentary.
☎ 09 220 48 02
▱ www.towncriers.be
✉ Graslei & Korenlei
€ €21 incl 2 *jenevers*

Yummy Walks (7, B2)
Take a guided 'Nibbling Through Ghent' walk (from 4pm to 6pm), tasting regional specialties with stops at traditional stores to try fine cheeses and meats, Belgian chocolates and confectionary, or do a 'Walk-ing Dinner Through Ghent' (6pm to 10pm) culinary walking tour that stops at four different restaurants for a course and drink at each restaurant.
☎ 0473 49 34 55
▱ www.vizit.be ✉ Crypt of Belfry € nibbling tour €10, dinner tour €45
☼ 3-5.30pm Sat

ARRIVAL & DEPARTURE
Air
The main international touch-down zone is **Brussels International Airport** (BRU; Zaventem Airport; 2, D2), located 13km northeast of the city centre. Brussels' second airport, **Brussels South Charleroi Airport** (CRL; 2, C3), is 46km southeast of the city and is serviced mainly by budget airlines Wizz Air (www.wizzair.com) and Ryanair (www.ryanair.com). Antwerp also has an airport, **Luchthaven Deurne** (ANR; 2, C1) that is mainly serviced by London City airport.

BRUSSELS INTERNATIONAL AIRPORT
The five-storey terminal building has restaurants, bars, a large cafeteria and many other facilities. Level 2 is the arrivals hall, where you'll be greeted by an information desk, a hotel reservations bureau, an ATM and currency exchange and car-hire counters. Level 3 is the departures hall.

Information
Flight information (☎ within Belgium 0900 700 00 €0.45 per minute, from abroad 02 753 77 53)
General enquiries (www.brusselsairport.be)
Parking (☎ 02 753 21 10)

Airport Access
From the train station located on Level -1 of the terminal building, the **Brussels Airport Express** (☎ Airport Station 02 753 24 40, general enquiries 02 528 28 28) runs approximately four times an hour from 5.12am, with the last train leaving at 0.20am to Brussels' Gare Centrale (22 minutes) and Gare du Midi (30 minutes). The trip costs €4.10/2.60 one way (1st/2nd class).

A private company, **MVIB/STIB** (☎ 02 515 20 00; www.stib.irisnet.be in French & Dutch) runs express buses (line 12) from the airport to Schuman metro station and from there to Gare Bruxelles-Luxembourg. The service runs regularly from 7am to 8pm

(outside these hours Schuman is the last stop), taking roughly 30 minutes. Tickets cost €3. **De Lijn** (☎ 02 526 28 20) runs bus 272 between the airport and Gare du Nord (€2.50, 45 minutes). There's also a direct bus service to Antwerp, from 7am to 11pm (☎ 32 52 33 40 00; €8; 50 minutes). All buses leave from level 0.

A taxi to the Lower Town will cost around €30. **Taxi Hendriks** (☎ 02 752 98 00) have taxis that are wheelchair accessible.

BRUSSELS SOUTH CHARLEROI AIRPORT
Information
Flight information (☎ 07 125 12 11)
General enquiries (www.charleroi-airport.com)

Airport Access
Buses to the airport (€10.50 one way) are based around departure times and leave Gare du Midi just over two hours before flight departure. Buses to Gare du Midi leave around half an hour after flight arrivals.

Bus
Brussels is well connected by long-distance bus to the rest of Europe, including the UK. **Eurolines** (www.eurolines.com) has a **main office** (3, E1; ☎ 02 274 13 50; Place Solvay 4, Schaerbeek; ☽ 9am-6pm Mon-Fri) beside Gare du Nord, where most buses leave from. A second **Eurolines office** (3, B6; ☎ 02 538 20 49; Ave Fonsny 13, St-Gilles; ☽ 9.30am-5.30pm Mon-Fri, 9.30am-4pm Sat) is opposite Gare du Midi. Eurolines also services **Ghent** (☎ 09 220 90 24; Koningin Elisabethlaan 73) and **Antwerp** (8, E2; ☎ 03 233 86 62; Van Stralenstraat 8).

Train
National train services are managed by **Belgian Railways** (NMBS/SNCB; ☎ 02 528 28 28; www.b-rail.be), whose logo is a 'B' in an oval. There are four levels of service: InterCity (IC) trains, which are the fastest; InterRegional (IR) trains; local (L) trains; and

peak-hour (P) commuter services stopping at specific stations. There's usually an IC or IR train departing every hour or half an hour to each of Belgium's other prime destinations (eg Antwerp, Bruges and Ghent). All trains have 1st- and 2nd-class carriages with both smoking and nonsmoking sections. Each of Brussels' main stations – **Gare du Nord** (3, E1), **Gare Centrale** (3, D4) and **Gare du Midi** (3, A6) – has an information office.

Gare du Midi is the main station for international travel. **Thalys** (www.thalys.com) operates high-speed trains connecting Brussels to destinations in France (including Paris in 1½ hours), the Netherlands, Germany and Switzerland; see the website for information and bookings. These trains also pass through Bruges, Antwerp and Ghent. **Eurostar** (www.eurostar.com) shuttles travellers between Brussels and London's Waterloo station via the Channel Tunnel in two hours, 30 minutes (eight to 10 services daily); the website details the plethora of fares available.

Antwerp to Bruges (fare €12.40; ☒ 1hr 20min, 2 per hr)

Antwerp to Ghent (fare €7.80; ☒ 50min, 2 per hr)

Bruges to Ghent (fare €5.40; ☒ 25min, 4 per hr)

Brussels to Antwerp (fare €6; ☒ 35min, 2 per hr)

Brussels to Bruges fare (€11.80; ☒ 60min, 2 per hr)

Brussels to Ghent (fare €7.40; ☒ 40min, 2 per hr)

Travel Documents
PASSPORT
Your passport must be valid for another three months beyond your stay – check with your local embassy for the latest passport information.

VISA
Citizens of the UK, US, Canada, Australia and most European nations, as well as a number of other countries, do not require a visa for stays of up to three months.

Customs & Duty Free
Duty-free goods are no longer sold to those travelling from one EU country to another. For goods purchased in airports or on ferries outside the EU, the usual allowances apply: 200 cigarettes, 50 cigars or 250g of loose tobacco; 1L of spirits plus 2L of wine; 50ml of perfume; and other goods to a value of €175. If you're a non-EU resident you can get the VAT (sales tax) back if you shop at stores with the 'Tax-Free Shopping' sticker, where it's (relatively) easy to request the relevant form to reclaim the VAT when leaving the EU.

Left Luggage
The 24-hour lockers on level 0 at Brussels airport cost between €5 and €7.50, depending on their size. Oversized luggage can also be left for a charge of €7.50 for up to three pieces. Similar lockers in each of Brussels' train stations cost between €2 and €3.25. In Bruges, the train station has lockers. In Antwerp, Centraal Station has both lockers and a left-luggage office (6am-11pm). Expect to pay between €1.50 and €3.30 per 24 hours.

GETTING AROUND
Brussels
Brussels has an extensive, efficient and easy-to-use public transport system, comprising the ultrareliable metro, trams, the *premetro* (trams that go underground for part of their journey) and buses. Public transport generally runs from 5.30am to 11pm or midnight daily and is managed by the **STIB** (MIVB in Dutch; ☎ 02 515 20 00; www.stib.irisnet .be), with main agencies at Ave de la Toison d'Or 15 (3, E6), Gare du Midi, and the Rogier (3, D2) and Porte de Namur (3, E5) metro stations. In this book, the nearest metro station is noted after the Ⓜ icon at the end of each listing. Where a *premetro* station is closer, it's noted after the 🚋 icon.

CAR & MOTORCYCLE
On a short trip to Brussels you're unlikely to need your own wheels and for the most part, seeing it on foot is far more fun. The

driving isn't bad – apart from the fact that you appear to be required by law to intimidate pedestrians even when they have right of way. Even if you're doing Bruges, Antwerp and Ghent in the one trip, the trains are fast, regular and good value. However, if you do need to hire a vehicle you could try **Budget** (☎ 02 753 21 70; www.budget .be) or **Europcar** (☎ 02 348 92 12; www .europcar.be), with desks at the airport.

METRO
Brussels' metro system has been operating since 1965, with its stations embellished by scores of works of art (ask the STIB for a brochure). There are three lines: Line 1A (yellow) goes from Roi Baudouin station to Herrmann-Debroux; Line 1B (red) runs from Erasme to Stockel; and Line 2 (orange) loops around from Simonis to Clémenceau. Stations are marked by rectangular signs with a white 'M' on a blue background.

TAXI
Taxis are metered, expensive and driven pugnaciously. Taxes and tips are officially included in the meter price. The basic tariff is €2.35, plus €1.15 per kilometre within the Brussels region and €2.28 per kilometre outside it. Between 10pm and 6am, an extra €1.85 is charged per trip. If you need a cab, ring **Taxi Verts** (☎ 02 349 49 49; www.taxis.be).

TRAM, PREMETRO & BUS
Before negotiating the city's extensive tram and bus network, pick up STIB's free transport map. *Premetro* trams run mainly underneath the boulevards running between Gare du Nord and Gare du Midi, but also duck down out of sight at other places around town.

TRAVEL PASSES & TICKETS
Tickets allowing access to all forms of public transport are available from vending machines in metro stations, from STIB kiosks and some newsagents, and on buses and trams. The best travel pass for visitors doing the sights is the Brussels Card (p19).

If you don't need the Brussels Card, a single-journey ticket on public transport is valid for one hour and costs €1.50; five/10-journey tickets cost €6.70/10.50. Day tickets (€4) are great value if you'll be jumping on and off public transport all day. You need to validate your ticket at the start of your trip in the machines located at the entrance to metro platforms or inside buses and trams.

Bruges
Much of the joy of visiting Bruges is just wandering the streets and if you've followed our accommodation recommendations, you really won't need public transport apart from getting to and from the train station. A network of buses operate in Bruges and to take one from the train station to the city centre, board any bus marked 'Centrum'. A single fare is €1. Taxis are generally waiting at the bus station and the Markt. To book a taxi in Bruges, phone ☎ 050 33 44 44 or ☎ 050 38 46 60.

A popular way of seeing the sights in Bruges is by bicycle, especially during the warmer months. The best bicycles to rent (and you need a good one for those bumpy streets!) are at **e-kar** (1, C2; ☎ 050 33 00 34; www.e-kar.com; Vlamingstraat 44-48).

Antwerp
Antwerp has a good network of buses, trams and *premetro* (a tram that runs underground at some stage of the journey), although many times you'll actually find it faster to walk and most locals use it to travel further than what you'll need as a visitor. Tickets are €1 and valid for an hour on all transport. The main tram and *premetro* stops are at Centraal Station (8, F3) and Groenplaats (8, B3). Taxis wait at Groenplaats and outside Centraal Station, otherwise call **Antwerp Taxi** (☎ 03 238 38 38). For bike hire (in the warmer months) try **De Windroos** (8, A2; ☎ 03 480 93 88; Steenplein 1a).

Ghent

Ghent's trams service the city centre al-though it's unlikely you'll need it. Tickets are €1 and valid for an hour. Bicycles are a fun alternative to walking the city centre. Bikes can be hired either from the train sta-tion or from **Biker** (7, A2; 09 224 29 03; Steendam 16).

PRACTICALITIES
Business Hours

Generally, shops are open from 8.30am or 9am until 5.30pm or 6pm Monday to Satur-day. Banks tend to open from 9am to 4pm or 5pm weekdays and Saturday morning, while post offices open from 9am to 5pm or 6pm weekdays and Saturday until noon. It's not unusual, however, to turn up at a shop fifteen minutes before closing time and find it already locked up. Many small boutiques and the like keep odd hours, so look at the opening times in the shopping chapters. Many of these shops are closed on Monday morning.

Climate & When to Go

The mild climate of the destinations cov-ered in this book are characterised by lots of grey, rainy weather. The warmest months are July and August, though they can also be the wettest. Weather-wise, the best months (but we offer no guarantees!) to visit are usually April/May and September. The weather is fickle and in winter you can head out under a perfect blue sky only to have it snow half an hour later, so be pre-pared for anything. Major events and fes-tivals (see p43 for Brussels, p70 for Bruges, p87 for Antwerp and p94 for Ghent) are generally held outside the winter months.

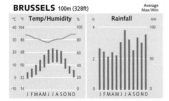

Costs

The prices in the eating chapters indicate the cost of a main course for one person.

€	up to €10
€€	€11 to €18
€€€	€19 to €28
€€€€	over €28

The prices in the sleeping chapters indicate the cost per night of a standard double room in high season.

Budget	under €85
Midrange	€85 to €149
Top end	€150 to €350
Deluxe	over €350

Disabled Travellers

Belgium is not exactly a world leader when it comes to accessibility for travellers with mobility problems, with many uneven or cobbled streets, street-level eateries with stairs at the entrance and few hotels with truly adequate facilities for the vision-impaired or those in wheelchairs. Many museums and theatres, however, have wheelchair access, while all train stations have wheelchair ramps (at least in Brus-sels). Many of Brussels' metro stations have Braille plaques at the entrance, but the only central station that's accessible by wheel-chair is Arts-Loi (3, F4). Whether travelling by train or visiting a theatre or museum, always give advance notice of the need to accommodate a wheelchair. **Taxi Hendriks** (☎ 02 752 98 00) provides a taxi service for disabled people.

Listings in this book that are wheelchair-friendly are marked by the ♿ icon and rated from 'fair' to 'excellent', with 'fair' meaning a minimal level of accessibility.

Discounts

Many of Belgiums' attractions and enter-tainment venues offer discounts for stu-dents and children, though family rates are rare. Students will need to produce an International Student Identity Card (ISIC) in order to qualify for reduced admission to museums and other sights, cinema tickets and train fares. The official 'over 55' cards, which Belgian senior citizens use to obtain concessions, are not available to foreigners, but elderly tourists may find themselves being given a discount anyway; disabled visitors face a similar situation where concessions apply.

The Brussels Card provides free admission to 25 museums and unlimited use of public transport – see p19. For more on museum freebies, see the boxed text on p78.

Electricity
Cycle AC
Frequency 50Hz
Plugs Two round pins, adaptors widely available
Voltage 220V

Embassies
Australia (3, F4; ☎ 02 286 05 00; www .austemb.be; 5th fl, Rue Guimard 6-8, Upper Town)
Canada (☎ 02 741 06 11; www.dfait-maeci.gc.ca/canada-europa/brussels/; Ave Tervuren 2, Etterbeek)
France (3, F3; ☎ 02 548 87 11; www .ambafrance-be.org in French & Dutch; Rue Ducale 65, Upper Town)
Germany (☎ 02 774 19 11; Ave de Tervuren 190, Etterbeek)
Netherlands (☎ 02 679 17 11; www .nederlandseambassade.be in French & Dutch; Ave Herrmann-Debroux 48, Auderghem)
New Zealand (3, F5; ☎ 02 512 10 40; www.nzembassy.com; 7th fl, Square de Meeûs 1, Upper Town)
UK (3, F4; ☎ 02 287 62 11; www.british embassy.gov.uk; Rue d'Arlon 85, EU Area)
US (3, F4; ☎ 02 508 21 11; www.usemb assy.be; Blvd du Régent 27, Upper Town)

Emergencies
The cities that are covered in this book are very safe to walk around, day or night, and the biggest hassle you're likely to face is the unwanted attention of a pickpocket when you're at a crowded popular sight, markets or train stations. Generally, the biggest danger to your safety here is not reading the label stating the percentage of alcohol in your beer. That, or slipping on dog doo.
Ambulance (☎ 100)
Fire (☎ 100)
Police (☎ 101)
Police (☎ 02 279 79 07) Nonemergency, Brussels
Rape Crisis Line (☎ 02 534 36 36) Brussels

Fitness
Bike riding – especially in Bruges, Antwerp and Ghent – doubles as both transport and a way to stay fit. The parks of each city also have their fair share of joggers, rain or shine. In Brussels, if you need to hit the gym, you can try the following places:
John Harris Fitness (4, F3; ☎ 02 219 82 54; www.johnharrisfitness.com; 7th fl, Radisson SAS, Rue du Fossé aux Loups 47, Lower Town; ☼ 6.30am-10pm Mon-Fri, 10am-7pm Sat & Sun)
Passage FitnessFirst (3, D2; ☎ 02 274 29 20; www.passagefitness.be in French & Dutch; Ave de Boulevard 21, St-Josse; ☼ 7am-10pm Mon & Tue, 9am-10pm Wed-Fri, 10am-6pm Sat & Sun) Branches in Ghent and Antwerp as well.

Gay & Lesbian Travellers
Attitudes to homosexuality have become less conservative in Brussels in recent years, evidenced by a burgeoning gay bar/club population around Rue du Marché au Charbon (4, B6). Brussels has a Gay and Lesbian Film Festival (www.fglb.org), now over 21 years old, an active sports club (www.bgs.org), an English-speaking gay club (http://geocities.com/eggbrus sels/) and a Belgian Lesbian and Gay Pride parade (www.blgp.be) held in May. For the latest information on what's happening while you're in town, the city's best

gay and lesbian meeting place is Rainbow House (p49) which doubles as a lively café. For information on just about every aspect of lesbian, bisexual and gay life, visit the excellent LesBiGayBrussels (www .lesbigaybrussels.be) website. In Antwerp Het Roze Huis (The Pink House; www.het rozehuis.be) has a good listing of events on in town.

Health
IMMUNISATIONS
There are no specific vaccination require-ments for Belgium.

MEDICAL SERVICES
Belgium has an excellent, extensive health-care system, and most doctors speak English. EU citizens are eligible for free emergency medical care (if they have an E111 certificate), but everyone else should organise medical insurance or be prepared to pay.

Brussels
A hospital with a 24-hour accident and emergency department is **Hôpital St-Pierre** (3, C6; ☎ 02 535 31 11; Rue Haute 322, Marolles). You can contact on-call doctors and pharmacists (day or night) on ☎ 02 479 18 18.

There are **Multipharma** outlets with long opening hours at Rue du Marché aux Poulets 37 (4, C4; ☎ 02 511 35 90), Place de la Monnaie 10 (4, D3; ☎ 02 217 43 88) and Rue Royale 178 (3, E3; ☎ 02 217 43 73), all in or near the Lower Town. Out-of-hours services are listed in pharmacy windows. The Dutch word for pharmacy is *apotheek*.

Bruges
Akademisch Ziekenhuis St-Jan (AZ Sint-Jan; ☎ 050 45 21 11; Ruddershove 10) is the city's main hospital and has a 24-hour emergency service. **Apotheek Dryepondt** (1, D3; ☎ 050 33 64 74; Wollestraat 7) is a good pharmacy.

Antwerp
Sint-Elisabethgasthuis (☎ 03 234 41 11; Leopoldstraat 26) is a central hospital with 24 hour service. **Apotheek Lotry** (8, B2; ☎ 03 233 01 86; Grote Markt 56) is a central pharmacy.

Ghent
Apotheek Evrard (7, B2; ☎ 09 223 27 08; Korte Munt 6) is a centrally located pharmacy.

PRECAUTIONS
Although Belgium has a poor environmen-tal record, which includes the pumping of sewage straight into the Senne river and extravagant waste production, the stand-ard of living in Belgium is generally quite high, so health precautions such as boiling tap water to make it safe for drinking are not necessary.

Holidays
1 January New Year's Day
March/April Easter Monday
1 May Labour Day
40th day after Easter Ascension Day
7th Sunday/Monday after Easter Whit Sunday/Monday
21 July Belgium National Day
15 August Assumption
1 November All Saints' Day
11 November Armistice Day
25 December Christmas

Internet
While Belgium is a computer-literate coun-try, you will find that Internet cafés are thin on the ground here. However, an increas-ing number of hotels have wi-fi (even midrange hotels and some B&Bs), so you'll be in good shape if you have a wi-fi ena-bled device as there's wi-fi everywhere – and some of it free. Visit www.jiwire.com to find your nearest hotspot – and yes, we realise the irony in telling someone to visit a website if they're looing for a wi-fi hotspot…

INTERNET CAFÉS

2Zones (8, C2; 03 232 24 00; Wolstraat 15, Antwerp; 11am-midnight)
Coffee Link (1, C6; 050 34 99 73; Mariastraat 38, Bruges; 11am-6pm Thu-Tue)
Coffeelounge (7, B2; 09 329 39 11; Botermarkt 9, Ghent; 10am-7pm Wed-Mon)
easyeverything (4, D2; Place de Brouckère 9, Brussels; 9am-midnight)

INTERNET SERVICE PROVIDERS

Belgium's largest ISP is **Skynet** (☎ 02 706 13 11; www.skynet.be in French & Dutch), which is operated by the national telecommunications giant Belgacom.

USEFUL WEBSITES

The Lonely Planet website (www.lonely planet.com) offers a speedy link to many of Belgium's websites. Other sites to try include:

Belgium for Beer Lovers (www.visit belgium.com/beer.htm) Treat this as research for your trip!
Brussels (www.brucity.be) Official website with information on transport, sights and activities, culture, business, the EU and more.
Use-it (www.use-it.be) The 'tourist office for young people', offers often funny, irreverent info on Ghent and Antwerp.
Noctis (www.noctis.com) For fresh clubbing news and to check whether you're on the party pics pages.
Golden Pages (www.pagesdor.be) In Belgium the Yellow pages are Gold.

Lost Property

To contact 'lost and found' at Brussels Airport, dial ☎ 02 753 68 20. If you lose something on the public transport network, contact **STIB** (☎ 02 515 23 94); for losses on the railway call the **Belgian Railways** (☎ 02 528 28 28).

Metric System

Belgium uses the metric system. Decimals are indicated with commas, thousands with

TEMPERATURE
$°C = (°F - 32) \div 1.8$
$°F = (°C \times 1.8) + 32$

DISTANCE
1in = 2.54cm
1cm = 0.39in
1m = 3.3ft = 1.1yd
1ft = 0.3m
1km = 0.62 miles
1 mile = 1.6km

WEIGHT
1kg = 2.2lb
1lb = 0.45kg
1g = 0.04oz
1oz = 28g

VOLUME
1L = 0.26 US gallons
1 US gallon = 3.8L
1L = 0.22 imperial gallons
1 imperial gallon = 4.55L

points (full stops). In Flemish shops, 250g is called a *half pond* and 500g a *pond*.

Money
ATMS

ATMs are becoming more widespread around the cities and you won't have too much trouble finding one that can handle Visa, MasterCard, Plus or Cirrus cards. You should however, make a note of how much you will be charged by your bank for cash transactions and especially advances on credit cards.

CHANGING MONEY

Easy places to change money are banks and foreign-exchange bureaus (*bureaux de change* in French, *wisselkantoren* in Dutch). Banks charge around €1.50 commission on currency transactions, while exchange bureaus usually have better rates but higher fees.

Camrail Exchange (3, A6; ☎ 02 556 36 00; Gare du Midi, St-Gilles, Brussels)
Europabank (☎ 09 221 00 31; train station, Ghent)
Goffin (8, B2; ☎ 03 232 20 56; Suikerrui 36, Antwerp)
ING Bank (1, C3; ☎ 050 44 45 40; Markt 19, Bruges)

CLOTHING & SHOE SIZES

Women's Clothing

Aust/UK	8	10	12	14	16	18
Europe	36	38	40	42	44	46
Japan	5	7	9	11	13	15
USA	6	8	10	12	14	16

Women's Shoes

Aust/USA	5	6	7	8	9	10
Europe	35	36	37	38	39	40
France only	35	36	38	39	40	42
Japan	22	23	24	25	26	27
UK	3½	4½	5½	6½	7½	8½

Measurements approximate only;
try before you buy.

Men's Clothing

Aust	92	96	100	104	108	112
Europe	46	48	50	52	54	56
Japan	S	M	M		L	
UK/USA	35	36	37	38	39	40

Men's Shirts (Collar Sizes)

Aust/Japan	38	39	40	41	42	43
Europe	38	39	40	41	42	43
UK/USA	15	15½	16	16½	17	17½

Men's Shoes

Aust/UK	7	8	9	10	11	12
Europe	41	42	43	44½	46	47
Japan	26	27	27.5	28	29	30
USA	7½	8½	9½	10½	11½	12½

CREDIT CARDS

Most credit cards are widely accepted. However, many small eateries do not accept credit cards and we've noted these in the reviews. For cancellations or assistance, call **American Express** (☎ 02 676 21 21), **MasterCard** (☎ 0800 150 96) or **Visa** (☎ 0800 183 97). Debit cards are increasingly accepted in Belgium. Endearingly, the Belgians, like the French, still love to write cheques – and they even get accepted.

CURRENCY

The unit of currency in Belgium is the euro, made up of 100 cents. There are notes of €500, €200, €100, €50, €20, €10 and €5, and coins in denominations of €2, €1 and 50, 20, 10, five, two and one cents.

TRAVELLERS CHEQUES

These are not common currency in Belgium, which prefers cold hard euro cash or the feel of plastic. The office of **American Express** (☎ 02 676 21 21; Blvd du Souverain 100, Watermael-Boitsfort) is well outside the city centre.

Newspapers & Magazines

Given the huge expat community, there's no shortage of international newspapers and magazines on the shelves, including most of the common ones from the UK and US. The widely available English-language magazine the **Bulletin** (www.ackroyd.be) is published on Thursday and has national news and a national entertainment guide. Ackroyd publishing also produce some handy expat publications.

Photography & Video

There's no shortage of supplies of good old-fashioned film and processing places in Belgium and for digital imaging supplies (batteries, memory cards etc), it's convenient to head to FNAC (p27). Don't expect to come home with (or post to your website) lots of brightly lit shots or videos – the weather is a fickle beast. Make hay while the sun shines. Local video and TV operate on the PAL system that predominates in Europe and Australia, but isn't compatible with the US NTSC or French SECAM systems. Remember when purchasing DVDs that you might need to check the region code to make sure the DVD will play when you get home.

Post

Belgium's **La Poste** (www.laposte.be) is very efficient and reliable and their website offers very easy to read information – including a postage calculator for parcels – in English (as well as French and Dutch, of course).

Brussels' **main post office** (4, D3; ☎ 02 226 39 00; Blvd Anspach, Lower Town) is on the 1st floor of the Centre Monnaie. There are other convenient branches at **Gare du Midi** (3, B6) and **Gare du Nord** (3, E1) and you can find others in your area easily by using their website.

In Bruges, the **main post office** (1, D3; ☎ 050 471 312; Markt 5) is the most convenient. In Antwerp, the **main post office** (8, B3; ☎ 03 202 69 11; Groenplaats 43) is handy to the Grote Markt. And in Ghent, the **main post office** (☎ 09 269 27 50; Lange Kruisstraat 55) is south of the centre of town. All these post offices are open Monday to Friday and Saturday morning.

POSTAL RATES
There are two rates for sending letters: *prioritaire* (priority) and *non-prioritaire* (nonpriority). Within Belgium, letters weighing less than 50g cost €0.52/0.46 priority/nonpriority; for letters to other European countries it's €0.70/0.60 and to the rest of the world it's €0.80/0.65.

Radio
Musique 3 (91.2FM; www.musiq3.be) Classical music.
Radio 21 (93.2FM; www.classic21.be) 'Classic' rock music.
VRT1 (91.7FM; www.radio1.be) News, talk and sport.
VRT2 (93.7FM; www.radio2.be) Oldies, top 40.

Telephone
Calls to anywhere within Belgium cost €0.05 per minute during peak time (8am to 7pm Monday to Friday) and €0.03 per minute during off-peak time. Most numbers prefixed with 0900 or 070 are pay-per-minute calls, while those preceded by 0800 are free calls. Phone booths are widespread and take a mixture of coins, phone cards and credit cards. A central **Belgacom** sales office (4, D3; ☎ 02 223 32 29, 0800 338 00; www.belgacom.be) is at Place de la Monnaie 9.

COUNTRY & CITY CODES
The country code for Belgium is ☎ 32. Brussels' old area code (02) has been incorporated into local phone numbers. The area code for Bruges is ☎ 050, Antwerp ☎ 03 and Ghent ☎ 09.

MOBILE PHONES
Belgium uses GSM 900/1800, compatible with the rest of Europe and Australia, but not with the systems used in North America or Japan. Belgacom outlets can provide phones, SIM cards and accessories. Currently, the best deals for SIM cards are offered by Proximus (www.proximus .be), who offer a Pay&Go SIM for €25 and you'll see offices for the service all over every town covered in this book. Mobile numbers begin with 0475 to 0479, 0486 or 0496.

PHONECARDS
A variety of fixed-value and rechargeable phonecards enabling local and international calls are available from Belgacom Téléboutiques, post offices and newsagents.

USEFUL PHONE NUMBERS
International direct dial code (☎ 00)
International directory inquiries (☎ 1405) In English
International operator (☎ 1324, 1224)
Local directory inquiries (☎ 1405)
Time (☎ 1300 in French, 1200 in Dutch)

Television
Cable TV is huge here (an estimated 95% of the population are hooked up), providing access to international networks such as BBC (1 and 2), CNN and MTV, and dozens of other channels. Some of the Dutch-language TV stations regularly broadcast English-language TV series and movies – usually with subtitles, sometimes amusingly dubbed.

Time

Belgium runs on Central European Time (GMT/UTC plus one hour). Daylight-savings time is in place from the last Sunday in March to the last Sunday in October.

Tipping

Tipping is not obligatory, as service and value-added tax (VAT) are included in hotel and restaurant prices, but go ahead if you appreciate the service.

Toilets

The charge for using public toilets varies between €0.30 and €0.50, payable to the attendant. The rather discriminatory street toilets (only for men, like the one at Église Ste-Catherine – 4, B2 – in Brussels) that you'll see on the streets are handy for guys who need to make a call of nature and incredibly gross to just about everyone else.

Tourist Information
BRUSSELS

Brussels International Tourism Office (4, D5; ☎ 02 513 89 40; www.brussels international.be; Hôtel de Ville, Grand Place; 🕑 9am-6pm) has plenty of information specific to Brussels and occasionally helpful service. Around the corner is the combined office of the **Flemish and Walloon tourist authorities** (4, D5; ☎ 02 504 03 90; www.opt.be, www.visitflanders.com; Rue du Marché aux Herbes 63; 🕑 9am-6pm Mon-Sat, 9am-1pm Sun Nov-Apr; 9am-6pm Mon-Fri, 9am-1pm & 2-6pm Sat & Sun May, Jun, Sep & Oct; 9am-7pm Mon-Fri, 9am-1pm & 2-7pm Sat & Sun Jul & Aug), which has some information on Brussels but concentrates more on national tourism.

BRUGES

The tourist office has moved from its convenient location in the centre of town to the most contentious building in the city, the **Concertgebouw** (1, A6; ☎ 050 44 46 46; www.brugge.be; 't Zand 34 🕑 10am-6pm Fri-Wed, to 8pm Thu).

ANTWERP

Tourism Antwerp (8, B2; 🕑 03 232 01 03; www.visitantwerp.be; Grote Markt 13; 🕑 9am-5.45pm Mon-Sat, 9am-4.45pm Sun & holidays) has fantastic free information, but the best stuff costs €1 to €2.

GHENT

Ghent's **tourist office** (7, B2; 🕑 09 232 01 03; www.visitgent.be; Botermarkt 17; 🕑 9.30am-6.30pm Apr-Oct, 9.30am-4.30pm Nov-Mar) is in a central location.

Women Travellers

Women should encounter few problems in Brussels, Bruges, Antwerp or Ghent as Belgium is a very reserved country. Locals are usually more than willing to assist anyone who's being hassled – which is rare.

LANGUAGE

Belgium's three main languages are Flemish, French and German. Flemish speakers occupy Flanders, the northern half of the country, and French speakers live in Wallonia in the south.

While travelling around Belgium you'll have to get used to switching between Flemish (a form of Dutch) and French. For example, when driving from Antwerp, the sign to Bergen (the Flemish name) will disappear and Mons (French) will appear. With the exception of Brussels, road signs, timetables and train stations signboards are written in the local language only, so you'll need to know city names in both languages. In Brussels, tourists can get by with English most of the time.

In both languages there's a polite and an informal version of the English 'you'. In Flemish the polite form is *u*, the informal is *je*. As a general rule, people who are older than you should be addressed as *u*. In French *tu* is used when addressing children and people you know well. *Vous* should be used with adults unless the person invites you to use *tu*. Only the polite forms are given here.

For more extensive coverage of Dutch/Flemish and French, get a copy of Lonely Planet's *Europe Phrasebook*.

In the following section, Dutch/Flemish phrases are given first, followed by the French.

Useful Words & Phrases

Hello.	*Dag/Hallo.*	*Bonjour.*
Goodbye.	*Dag.*	*Au revoir.*
Yes.	*Ja.*	*Oui.*
No.	*Nee.*	*Non.*
Please.	*Alstublieft.*	*S'il vous plaît.*
Thank you (very much).	*Dank u (wel).*	*Merci (beaucoup).*
That's fine/You're welcome.	*Graag gedaan.*	*Je vous en prie.*
Excuse me.	*Excuseer mij.*	*Excusez-moi.*
I'm sorry.	*Pardon.*	*Pardon.*
Do you speak English?	*Spreekt u Engels?*	*Parlez-vous anglais?*
I don't understand.	*Ik begrijp het niet.*	*Je ne comprends pas.*

Getting Around

What time does the ... leave?	*Hoe laat vertrekt ...?*	*À quelle heure part ...?*
What time does the ... arrive?	*Hoe laat komt ... aan?*	*À quelle heure arrive ...?*
train	*de trein*	*le train*
bus	*de bus*	*le bus*
boat	*de boot*	*le bateau*
plane	*het vliegtuig*	*l'avion*
Where is the (ticket office)?	*Waar is (het loket)?*	*Où est (le guichet)?*
Which platform does it depart from?	*Vanaf welk spoor vertrekt het?*	*Il part de quel quai?*
(Go) straight ahead.	*(Ga) rechtdoor.*	*(Continuez) tout droit.*
(Turn) left.	*(Ga) naar links.*	*(Tournez) à gauche.*
(Turn) right.	*(Ga) naar rechts.*	*(Tournez) à droite.*

Buying Tickets

I'd like ... ticket.	*Ik wil graag ...*	*Je voudrais un billet ...*
a one-way	*een enkele reis*	*simple*
a return	*een retourticket*	*aller et retour*
a 1st-class	*eerste klas*	*de première classe*
a 2nd-class	*tweede klas*	*de deuxième classe*

Accommodation

Do you have any rooms available?	*Heeft u een kamer vrij?*	*Est-ce que vous avez des chambres libres?*
I'd like (a) ...	*Ik wil graag een ...*	*Je voudrais ...*
single room	*eenpersoons-kamer*	*une chambre à un lit*
double room	*tweepersoons-kamer*	*une chambre avec un grand lit*
How much is it ...?	*Hoeveel is het ...?*	*Quel est le prix ...?*
per night	*per nacht*	*par nuit*
per person	*per persoon*	*par personne*

Shopping & Services

I'd like to buy ...	*Ik wil graag ... kopen.*	*Je voudrais acheter ...*
How much is it?	*Hoeveel is het?*	*C'est combien?*
May I look at it?	*Mag ik het zien?*	*Est-ce que je peux le voir?*
I don't like it.	*Ik vind het niet leuk.*	*Cela ne me plaît pas.*
more	*meer*	*plus*
less	*minder*	*moins*
smaller	*kleiner*	*plus petit*
bigger	*groter*	*plus grand*
Do you accept ...?	*Accepteert u ...*	*Est-ce que je peux payer avec ...?*
credit cards	*kredietkaarten*	*ma carte de crédit*
travellers cheques	*reischeques*	*des chèques de voyage*
I'm looking for ...	*Ik ben op zoek naar ...*	*Je cherche ...*
the bank	*de bank*	*une banque*
a bookshop	*een boekenwinkel*	*une librairie*
the chemist/pharmacy	*de drogist/apotheek*	*la pharmacie*
a laundry	*een wasserette*	*la blanchisserie*
the market	*de markt*	*le marché*
the police	*de politie*	*la police*
a public phone	*een telefooncel*	*une cabine téléphonique*
a public toilet	*een openbaar toilet*	*les toilettes*
a supermarket	*een supermarkt*	*un supermarché*
the tourist office	*de VVV*	*l'office de tourisme*

Emergencies

Help!	*Help!*	*Au secours!*
I'm ill.	*Ik ben ziek.*	*Je suis malade.*
Where is the hospital?	*Waar is het ziekenhuis?*	*Où est l'hôpital?*
I'm lost.	*Ik ben de weg kwijt.*	*Je me suis égaré/e. (m/f)*
Go away!	*Ga weg!*	*Allez-vous-en!*
Call ...!	*Haal ...*	*Appelez ...!*
a doctor	*een doktor*	*un médecin*
the police	*de politie*	*la police*

Time & Dates

What time is it?	*Hoe laat is het?*	*Quelle heure est-il?*
When?	*Wanneer?*	*Quand?*
in the morning	*'s morgens*	*du matin*
in the afternoon	*'s middags*	*de l'après-midi*
in the evening	*'s avonds*	*du soir*
today	*vandaag*	*aujourd'hui*
tomorrow	*morgen*	*demain*
Monday	*maandag*	*lundi*
Tuesday	*dinsdag*	*mardi*
Wednesday	*woensdag*	*mercredi*
Thursday	*donderdag*	*jeudi*

Friday	*vrijdag*	*vendredi*
Saturday	*zaterdag*	*samedi*
Sunday	*zondag*	*dimanche*

Numbers

0	*nul*	*zéro*	20	*twintig*	*vingt*
1	*één*	*un*	30	*dertig*	*trente*
2	*twee*	*deux*	40	*veertig*	*quarante*
3	*drie*	*trois*	50	*vijftig*	*cinquante*
4	*vier*	*quatre*	60	*zestig*	*soixante*
5	*vijf*	*cinq*	70	*zeventig*	*soixante-dix*
6	*zes*	*six*	80	*tachtig*	*quatre-vingts*
7	*zeven*	*sept*	90	*negentig*	*quatre-vingt-dix*
8	*acht*	*huit*	100	*honderd*	*cent*
9	*negen*	*neuf*	1000	*duizend*	*mille*
10	*tien*	*dix*	1,000,000	*miljoen*	*million*

EATING

ENTERTAINMENT

SLEEPING

FEATURES

Den Dyver	*Eating*
Pier 19	*Entertainment*
Limonada	*Drinking*
Cirio	*Café*
Musée Horta	*Highlights*
Verso	*Shopping*
Belfort	*Sights/Activities*
Erasmus	*Sleeping*
Canal Cruises	*Trips & Tours*

AREAS

	Beach, Desert
	Building
	Land
	Mall
	Other Area
	Park/Cemetery
	Sports
	Urban

HYDROGRAPHY

	River, Creek
	Intermittent River
	Canal
	Swamp
	Water

BOUNDARIES

	State, Provincial
	Regional, Suburb

ROUTES

	Tollway
	Freeway
	Primary Road
	Secondary Road
	Tertiary Road
	Lane
	Under Construction
	One-Way Street
	Unsealed Road
	Mall/Steps
	Tunnel
	Walking Path
	Walking Trail/Track
	Pedestrian Overpass
	Walking Tour

TRANSPORT

	Airport, Airfield
	Bus Route
	Cycling, Bicycle Path
	Ferry
	General Transport
	Metro
	Monorail
	Rail
	Taxi Rank
	Premetro, Tram

SYMBOLS

	Bank, ATM
	Buddhist
	Castle, Fortress
	Christian
	Diving, Snorkeling
	Embassy, Consulate
	Hospital, Clinic
	Information
	Internet Access
	Islamic
	Jewish
	Lighthouse
	Lookout
	Monument
	Mountain, Volcano
	National Park
	Parking Area
	Petrol Station
	Picnic Area
	Point of Interest
	Police Station
	Post Office
	Ruin
	Telephone
	Toilets
	Zoo, Bird Sanctuary
	Waterfall